An Invitation to the Spiritual Journey

John P. Gorsuch

Paulist Press ◆ New York/Mahwah

Acknowledgments

The Publisher gratefully acknowledges the use of the following materials: Excerpts from *The Collected Works of St. Teresa of Avila, Volume II* translated by Kieran Kavanaugh and Otilio Rodriguez, copyright © 1980 by the Washington Province of Discalced Carmelites, are reprinted by permission of ICS Publications/2131 Lincoln Road, N.E./Washington, D.C. 20002/U.S.A.; excerpts from *He Touched Me* by John Powell, S.J., copyright © 1974 by John Powell, S.J., are reprinted by permission of Tabor Publishing, a division of DLM, Inc., Allen Texas; excerpts from *Inviting the Mystic, Supporting the Prophet* by L. Patrick Carroll, S.J., and Katherine Marie Dyckman, S.N.J.M., copyright © 1981 by The Missionary Society of St. Paul the Apostle, are reprinted by permission of the Paulist Press; excerpts from *Living With Apocalypse: Spiritual Resources for Social Compassion* edited by Tilden Edwards, copyright © 1984 by the Shalem Institute for Spiritual Formation, Inc., are reprinted by permission of Harper & Row, Publishers, Inc.

Library of Congress Cataloging-in-Publication Data

Gorsuch, John P., 1932–
    An invitation to the spiritual journey / John P. Gorsuch.
      p. cm.
    Includes bibliographical references.
    ISBN 0-8091-3119-6
    1. Spiritual life—Anglican authors. I. Title.
BV4501.2.G65   1990
248.4′83—dc20
                                        89-39804
                                        CIP

Published by Paulist Press
997 Macarthur Boulevard
Mahwah, N.J. 07430

Printed and bound in the United States of America

CONTENTS

24630

ACKNOWLEDGMENTS

It's simply not possible to acknowledge and thank all those who, in some way, have contributed to the making of this book and to the Center for Spiritual Development in which much of what is written in these pages is put to the test, but here at least are some of those to whom I owe so much: My grandmother, "Kiki"; H. Richard Niebuhr; Tilden Edwards; Gerald May; Thomas Keating; Donald Walters; Asha Praver; R. Hugh Dickinson; the congregations I have served—especially the people of Epiphany Parish, Seattle; the hospitable deans of St. Mark's Cathedral, Seattle: Cabby Tennis and Fred Northup, and the cathedral staff and congregation; Susan Moseley, Eleanor Reed, Dick Cleveland, Willard Wright, Wylie Hemphill and other benefactors and board members of the Center; those who have attended and supported the Center's programs, classes, conferences and retreats and those who have come for spiritual direction who have taught me so much; office managers and allies Charlotte Goldman and Marjorie Jodoin; and most especially Beverly, Anne and Margaret Gorsuch.

It is my wife, Beverly, who has encouraged and joined me in the exploration of the spiritual process and who more than anyone has helped this book happen. Many of the things I consider best in these pages have been inspired and suggested by her experience, insight and support.

FOREWORD

It has been nearly a decade since I first met John Gorsuch. In those years, he and I have shared much of our explorations of the spiritual life. His journey has inspired mine as I have seen him claim and act upon his desire to seek a deeper and more direct conscious relationship with God, and to help others do the same. This book is clearly a manifestation of that journey.

In these pages, Jack shares the wisdom and the ways that have proven meaningful through years of experience. He knows whereof he speaks. The insights he expresses have been tested and refined in the crucible of his own prayer and ministry. This is not a pop catalog of psychospiritual gimmicks, but a coherent, integrated offering that invites us to a deeper, richer life with God and one another.

The words that Jack has written are *grounded*. They are grounded in good theology, in solid psychology, and in a realistic appraisal of the graces and confusions of modern daily life. They are grounded in the history of spirituality, and in scripture. And they are gounded in faith. Jack speaks of God's invitation for all of us to a deeper love, and of our ambivalence in responding to that call. He shares his own and others' struggles in moving from fear and doubt toward courage and trust. He does this in a way that is of solid, practical help.

The stories that he tells—and there are many of them— not only make for lively reading and clear understanding, but they also undergird this work with a solid incarnational foundation. From Martin Luther King to Teresa of Avila, from people in Jack's groups to Paramahansa Yogananda, these are stories of real persons; they apply to you and to me in our real lives, in our bodies and relationships, in our work and play. But never does this earthy and practical atmosphere cloud the transcendent mystery of God. Instead, it calls forth awe and wonder in the radiance of divine grace.

This integration of the incarnational and the transcendent is, I think, a mark of truth. Many things are written about spirituality these days. Most, in the name of healing the old body/mind/spirit dichotomy, so overemphasize the immanence of God that they reduce the Divine One to a psychic archetype, a cosmic energy resource, or an imaginary playmate. Some, going to the opposite extreme, so expound the absolute otherness of God that they overlook or even disparage the beauty and fundamental goodness of creation. Both of these errors, I feel, arise from thinking one's words and thoughts instead of praying them.

Jack Gorsuch's work is clearly grounded in prayer, and it rings true. It is a privilege, now, for me to let *An Invitation to the Spiritual Journey* speak for itself.

Gerald G. May
Shalem Institute for Spiritual Formation
Mount St. Alban
Washington, D.C. 20016

PREFACE

I don't have much technical information about lungfish but I like the idea of them. They are pioneers. We are alive today because some water-dwelling fish stuck their noses out of their element to breathe the larger atmosphere of air.

I think human beings are like lungfish and I think we are living in a lungfish time. I have been a clergyperson for over thirty years, but I don't know when I have been aware of more people who are looking into spiritual growth. They are coming out of the water and trying out their spiritual lungs. It feels to me like a special moment.

In 1985 I followed a dream about which I had been musing for a long time. I started the Center for Spiritual Development in Seattle, an ecumenical, non-profit corporation designed to help people explore, deepen and affirm the place of God in their lives without underestimating the challenges along the way. For some time I had wanted to begin a center to help persons of different denominations—and some who didn't go to any church—with their spiritual journeys. Other centers such as the Shalem Institute in Washington, D.C., where I had trained as a spiritual director, were beginning to make an impact, and I sensed the need for such a center where I live. More and more persons were seeking me out because they wanted to talk about becoming more attuned to God's presence and activity. Many were asking for specific classes on how to grow spiritually, especially for help with prayer and meditation and with how to get on with the journey in everyday life. I was aware, too, that churches were starting to ask for programs on spirituality, that retreat and conference centers were increasingly in demand, and that books on the spiritual life were being read widely. The timing seemed right.

What had led me to this step is, perhaps, a metaphor for

what has been going on for many people. I was someone who had gotten too busy for God. I had been rector of a large parish that had been involved in a number of relevant ministries, from social action to the enablement of lay ministry to women's ordination, and I had taught courses on the spiritual life and prayer in adult education classes with some success, but my own spiritual life was underdeveloped. When I prayed it was usually on the run, on my way to the hospital or with someone in need, but I told myself I had little prayer time available for myself. Like many persons who want to deepen their relationship with God but don't seem to get around to it except occasionally, I felt guilty. I knew that a relationship with God is like any relationship in the sense that it deepens as it is cultivated. And I knew that I couldn't show others the joy and beauty of God unless I experienced something of that myself.

In 1975 a friend and fellow Episcopal priest and I stood highest in the final balloting for the office of bishop in our diocese. When the last ballot was cast, I lost the election. I mourned. Moving into the episcopacy seemed to me like the outcome of a fairly fast run up the church chairs. Six months later another election, in another part of the country, was held. I was one of three finalists and had a strong sense that I might be elected. Before the convention to elect was held, I had a dream in which I was being vested in cope and miter. Just as the vesting was being finalized, cope and miter went up in smoke and the bishop-to-be was replaced by a new baby, filled with light. This dream, and some other issues I had been wrestling with, caused me to call the Search Committee. "I'm withdrawing my name," I told them. "You're crazy," they said. "You could be elected." "I probably am crazy," I said, thinking I really was, "but I'm pulling out."

So much in my culture, my childhood and my own inclinations had led me to this place. What was I doing by pulling out my name? Later, as the weeks passed, I found myself drawn again and again to talking to and reading about persons who had taken the spiritual journey another step. I reread *The Interior Castle* by St. Teresa, *The Testament of Devotion* by Thomas Kelly, and *The Autobiography of a Yogi* by Paramahansa Yogananda. I rediscovered Thomas Merton and became acquainted with Thomas Keating. I wished I could experience God as intimately as Brother Lawrence. I understood Tilden Edwards when he retold an old German story about the two hands of God—the right hand which took human form and the left hand which was empty, still searching for truth. "One cannot receive the fullness of the right hand except through the pilgrimage of the left,"[1] but if the left is already full it has no room to receive. I knew how cluttered my left hand had been. I had been stuffing myself with busyness, running myself ragged, taking myself so seriously, preoccupying myself with institutional achievements and personal successes. Some good things had been achieved, but I knew too little about that which I preached: the abundant life of the spirit.

Slowly, I began to take my spiritual journey more seriously. I was as busy as ever, but it became important to make room for God. I'm not sure anyone else could notice what was stirring within me, but I started to notice. Frequently as cluttered-up as always, a little space was nevertheless being made in me for a larger, more generous Life. In 1983 I was granted a sabbatical. I visited a Benedictine monastery in New Mexico. I learned deep meditation in a spiritual community in California. I began my training as a spiritual director at the Shalem Institute for Spiritual Formation in Washington, D.C. When I returned, people from several churches and people who didn't attend church began knocking on my door. They wanted to be in touch with God. In 1985 I launched the Center for Spiritual Development.

My story is not unusual. We are a cluttered people who often sincerely believe in God but just as often don't know how to contact God in an enduring kind of way. We usually only make stabs at trying to make room for the Divine. But the hunger is there. We are haunted by the notion that life is more than we live it out.

The thing about lungfish is that they stick their snouts out of water to try on air for size. It's not easy, and it may even seem unnatural. But once you breathe air, while you may go back to gills again and again, you can't be satisfied with anything less than air. Nothing tastes so sweet.

That's what spiritual development is like. We swim in water, but once we get a lungful of the good stuff, nothing else fills us. More and more people are discovering that their air is God. Joseph Campbell tells about walking off 51st Street and Fifth Avenue into St. Patrick's Cathedral in New York City.[2] He leaves one of the most economically conscious cities in the world and walks into a world that everywhere speaks of spiritual mysteries. The mystery of the cross and the stained glass windows take his consciousness to another level. Then he walks out and is back on the level of the street again. He wonders: Can he take the cathedral consciousness with him? Or, to use my metaphor, can the lungfish swim and breathe air at the same time?

So many people today want to breathe divine air as they live out their daily lives. In response to that desire in myself and others, I have written this little book as a way to address the most common themes I hear raised everywhere I go, during the classes we teach at the Center, and among the people I see in spiritual direction. There is a great desire for spiritual food these days and for practical books that will address the issues people experience when they take up the spiritual life as a real option. All of the things written about here have been written about in other places, I am sure, but I haven't seen anything that pulls them together in a plain, short way. When I travel to an area that is new to me, I like to buy a guidebook that will invite me to try out the sights and introduce me to the terrain. Those books don't cover everything, but they get me started.

While this book is primarily for Christians, it is also designed to be of general help. There are many people today who are interested in the spiritual life but are testing the waters regarding the church or are members of another tradition. For this reason some subjects dear to Christian spirituality, such as the sacraments and the church, are not elaborated upon here.

More than anything, I hope that this book will bring inner renewal and coax us closer to the splendor and love of God which is our true homeland.

The main thing about the spiritual journey is that it's worth it. There are a lot of human lungfish swimming around who know that.

MOVING OUT

This book was launched on a beautiful Indian summer afternoon. At first, I hadn't noticed. I was indoors, surrounded by books, paper, notes, manila folders. I was feeling pushed and anxious. I had vowed to take the afternoon off to dream about the book with Beverly, my wife. Both of us had left work and headed for home—she from her practice as a psychotherapist, I from the Episcopal Church of the Epiphany in Seattle where I was then the rector. There were new programs to launch, people needing attention, countless details that had to be attended to. I wanted to talk with her about writing a book, but it felt like a heavy project and I wondered if I could take on one more thing without going into overload.

"Why don't we work out in the backyard patio?" Bev suggested. I resisted. I wanted to get on with the business at hand—no time for frivolity. All of my notes and papers were on hand; I'd have to move them. There were so many issues to consider. How could a book on the spiritual life get into meaty stuff and still be simple and short? How could it get at the real issues people struggle with when they begin to lean more intentionally into their spiritual journeys? How should it be organized? What should it include?

I wanted to move outside and I resisted it. Somehow this little struggle seemed a metaphor of something else struggling in me. Finally the decision was made. Gathering up my materials, I joined Bev and we moved outdoors into a perfect day. The air sparkled. The temperature was in the mid-seventies. Bees were collecting the last pollen of the summer. The day flooded us with golden acceptance, seeping into muscle and bone until, almost in spite of ourselves, we began to relax.

It felt good to be together. We began to talk about our day, sharing our feelings. The sharing quite naturally led to note-taking, to writing.

That afternoon was complete in itself. It needed nothing to make it perfect. We were very productive. And the questions I wanted to address began to emerge. They were my questions; they were the questions of many people who had come to me over the years to explore whether the spiritual life was for them.

How do I find you, God? How do I learn to open myself to you? Can I really trust that you are as good as others have said you are and as I have sometimes experienced you to be? In what ways do I resist you? Is the journey deeper into your life alien to my deepest needs or an adventure into a truer part of myself as well as into you? Where will you take me?

I believe that my experience on that Indian summer day is a metaphor of the spiritual journey. God constantly floods us with his love and beckons us into a better place, but we often don't give it a chance. We make our excuses and tell ourselves we don't have time. Even as we yearn to move into the sun, we hold back. We keep busy, feeling somehow that if we fuss and obsess, we won't have to make space for God. We decide it is easier to surround ourselves with piles of work and worry and stew about decisions and problems than to move into something that holds better promise. Is it because we feel that if we were to move out, God might touch us, and if God touched us, we might have to change?

Still, we yearn to breath crystalline air and feel warm sun on our backs. I believe that most people want more of God in their lives. There is that in us which knows that nothing created on the face of the earth can ever satisfy us the way God can. We reach toward fame, power, money, beauty, sex and health, but we find that there is something in us that returns to that inner hunger which only God can satisfy because God put it there. Even if we don't know it is God we want, we sense that we need to be in touch with spiritual reality if we are to be complete. I find that even if people don't use "God talk" or say they don't believe in God, they talk about the centrality of spiritual things all the time. Some talk about the way nature gives them a sense of connectedness to the universe. Some describe how music helps them experience the oneness of things. Some talk about what a wondrous process it is to grow into a more integrated, individuated person and how they sense the hand of something intrinsically good at work in that process. However they describe spiritual reality, people know it when they see it and they yearn for more. There is that in human nature which is like a needle in a compass; we search for the spiritual dimension until we point north.

As Gerald May says:

> The desire for belonging and union, for loving and for just being can be seen collectively as the three basic facts of human spiritual longing. We are frustrated repeatedly in our attempts to ease this longing for two reasons: first, because we protect ourselves against the disappointment of being found wanting, and second, because we seek it solely in relationships to other people when in fact it must come as well from our relationship to the source of our existence in all of creation. In moments when the clouds of confusion clear and we can see our longing in perspective, it appears as a nagging knowledge that we come from somewhere and exist for some purpose. Our search, then, is a seeking for our deepest roots—not the roots of family, nor of race, nor even of the human species, but our roots as creatures of and in this cosmos.[1]

So the sun beckons. Still, for all of its golden promise we hold back. Sometimes we are afraid. Sometimes we are stubborn. Sometimes we give up too soon. We tell ourselves that a good thing like warm sun isn't for us after all—at least as an ongoing, normal part of living. How many of us there are who have had times when the things of the Spirit seemed very close but, after such moments pass, tell ourselves such things are rare and accidental or at least not something we can hope to experience in a sustained way. Or, seeing the lives of the great spiritual heroes, heroines and saints and our own lives by comparison, we tell ourselves we are phonies. Or, perceiving that the spiritual life is not an instant fix, we sigh and move on to other things. Or, too quickly dismissing the spiritual enterprise as irrelevant to real life, we hardly allow ourselves to linger over our longing for something deeper.

What is the spiritual life? Is it true it's not for people like us? Is it mainly for people who live in monasteries and caves or for those who are naturally more holy than the rest of us?

I don't believe that. The fact that human beings in every culture and generation seem to quest for God or something like God is for me one of those persistent clues that the spiritual life is for everyone. There are many kinds of religions, not all of them particularly grace-filled, but the word "religion" means *religio*, linking back. We are linked to the music of the spheres, and even the most deaf among us doesn't not hear something.

People ask me to define the spiritual life. I respond by saying I believe it's a stance toward life which believes every one of us is meant to wake up to so that more and more everything cries out "God" for us. As Thomas Merton says, we are part of a glorious cosmic dance which is always going on. It beats in the blood of all of us even if we don't know it. The purpose of the spiritual life is to help us learn how to remove the obstacles that stand between us and the union we already have with God. This means that we don't search for something that is foreign to us but uncover that which is already here.

I believe that St. Paul was exactly right when he said we live and move and have our being in the divine life. The holy is present to everybody, not just a few sanctified souls. In the great spiritual traditions of the world the image of waking from sleep is used to describe what happens when we become more aware, which means we don't have to go somewhere else or be someone else to get the Holy One's attention. We do, however, need to understand that our spiritual antennae are so full of static that we tune God out. If we could reduce the noise that is caused by what Thomas Keating calls our "false self system"—our hangups and distortions—we could begin to hear the great symphony of love that pours forth from the divine heart.

I believe that at some place deep within us most of us know how closely we are linked to Spirit. Granting there are plenty of questions in our time about whether the spiritual world even exists, I think that the real question is whether we want to uncover it. It's like the film "My Dinner with Andre" in which a man who has successfully passed through most of his mid-life issues returns to tell a friend what wonderful things he's learned. As they talk, Andre's friend can't (or won't) understand what Andre is saying. Andre has been in touch with a level of reality his friend is unwilling to follow. And yet, for all his lack of comprehension, he's not the complete stranger to Andre's truth he tells himself he is.

Plato said we are like people in a cave who face the back wall, perceiving only the shadows that are cast on that wall from an unknown source of light. Many of us seem to be content with shadows. At least we settle for shadows until we tire of such illusion or are finally forced by life or tragedy or our inner spiritual compasses to search for something better. Then we may turn around and move to the entrance of the cave where we see the reality which has been there all along.

I'm one of those people who loves to read good fantasy. Tolkien's *Lord of the Rings*, for example, speaks to me because it's so full of spiritual hints. Just behind Tolkien's words are images of a larger reality—a reality which is already part of me but which beckons me to enter more fully into mysteries I only sense. C.S. Lewis often does that for me, too. He believed we live in a kind of "shadowland" while still retaining a memory of what the universe really is at its heart. This is our home, and yet our homeland is bigger than we usually admit. Lewis was pretty clear that our amnesia is not entirely due to forgetfulness. There is that in us which chooses not to remember. In *The Great Divorce* Lewis takes his readers through a fanciful journey to the outskirts of heaven where souls are given the chance to leave hell and enter a glorious dimension of everlasting growth and spiritual adventure if they will forego whatever precious sin they hug to themselves. One of the things that makes that book so compelling is the way it describes how many souls willingly choose to travel back to hell because "There is always something they prefer to joy—that is, to reality."

> "Milton was right," said my Teacher. "The choice of every lost soul can be expressed in the words 'Better to reign in Hell than serve in Heaven.' There is always something they insist on keeping, even at the price of misery. . . . Ye see it easily enough in a spoiled child that would sooner miss its play and its supper than say it was sorry and be friends. Ye call it the Sulks. But in adult life it has a hundred fine names—Achilles' wrath and Coriolanus' grandeur, Revenge and Injured Merit and Self-Respect and Tragic Greatness and Proper Pride."[2]

Still, we want to find our way back to the real thing. We understand what the medieval mystic, Meister Eckhart, meant when he said, "God is at home. It is we who have gone out for a walk."

God, I believe, is deeply imprinted on our souls, even if we have smothered this imprint over by skepticism, or by our warding off of the potential disappointment we might feel lest it be found wanting, or are so terribly worn down by living that we can barely remember its possibility. John Eusden tells of a time he went on a retreat at which he arrived physically, emotionally and spiritually exhausted. He said he was estranged from those he loved most, had lost God and didn't feel very good about himself. His spiritual director took one look at him and brought him a collection of children's fairy tales, suggesting that he read them until he fell asleep.

Eusden said a common theme ran through all those tales: The main character, who is in reality royalty, is raised by another family than his own to think he's a nobody. When the child grows up he discovers his true identity. He comes home to the truth but the work has just begun; what follows is a long struggle with the forces of evil and one's shadows until finally the person is restored to himself and brings to his realm that wholeness he himself has uncovered.

Eusden fell asleep and dreamed that he, too, was royalty. He woke up rested and ready for the retreat. "My problem was not that I thought too highly of myself but that I did not think highly enough of myself. The next day, my director told me to imagine a host of angels going before me proclaiming, 'Make Way for the Image of God.' "[5]

We are all made in that image, we all come forth from a larger homeland. We are more than we know and are part of more than we admit.

This book is for people who are deciding to search out their spiritual homeland and their true identity. It comes out of my experience with many people over the years who want to connect at a deeper level with the divine power and presence and for whom theological abstractions are no longer enough. They want to experience the reality of God for themselves. It is not enough to hear about God second-hand. They are drawn to this journey but they are also usually uneasy about going too far with it because they're under no illusion that the spiritual journey is a band-aid. They know they are going to bump into the things about themselves they would rather not confront because this is a journey into fuller life, not a journey back to the womb on one hand or to unworldly heavens on the other. Uneasy or not they now see that the search for God is implicit in the human psyche and that it holds such great promise that it just can't be ignored any longer.

This search for communion with the living God is my own journey, and it was that for which I was reaching at deeper levels that first day Beverly and I discussed this book. At one level, I was wrestling with whether to leave a dark room for the warm sun. At another, I was engaged in an ongoing struggle to respond to or resist something even more profound—to be open to the Gracious Presence or to hug my own shadow.

As we shall see, the spiritual life is a life that includes invitation and resistance. The good news is that the sun keeps on shining, graciously inviting us to experience the golden acceptance only it knows how to give.

WHAT DRAWS US TO GOD?/ WHAT HOLDS US BACK?

Several years ago on the popular television program "The Muppet Show" three of the puppet characters were on a rocket ship hurtling through space. A loudspeaker announced sonorously: "In two minutes we will reach the end of the universe and then the meaning and purpose of life will be revealed to you!" The countdown began. The air was charged with excitement and expectation. Suddenly a bell clanged. The three muppets jumped. "What's that?" one said. "It's the dinner bell!" Then came a long pause; no one spoke. "What's for dinner?" someone finally asked. A response came from off camera: "Beef stew." "Hmmmm," a second muppet said. A few seconds passed and then he left for dinner. Soon the other two followed him. The control room was deserted. The space ship was approaching the end of the universe and the secret of life. But no one was there to receive the great revelation; they had all gone in for beef stew.

This little parable captures the feelings many of us carry with us when we start on the spiritual journey. On one hand, we are excited and eager as we draw nearer to the secrets of the universe. At the same time, we are cautious, even frightened. It doesn't take all that much to draw us away from our quest. Even a mediocre "beef stew" can do it.

Again and again I have found that for the spiritual life to prosper, it is important to acknowledge right at the beginning the tension that most of us feel between our attraction to the abundant life promised when we let go of that which is less than God, and our anxiety about what might happen to us if we get serious about opening ourselves more fully to the Holy One. This tension is very common. We want to develop a deeper relationship with God and yet we soon discover we have powerful resistances about moving too far. Reluctance to face into this issue can end in "beef stew" instead of real spiritual food.

If the spiritual life is going to take off, there is nothing more essential to look at in the initial stages of that journey than what draws us to God and what holds us back.

It isn't difficult to get in touch with what draws us to God. If we have even been touched for a moment by God's presence in nature or people or church or through some compelling experience, we know we want more of a good thing. Over a period of time I have compiled a list of those things which most commonly seem to draw people to God. Some most frequently mentioned are:

Peace

A sense of oneness with the depths of life

Hope

Awareness of the beauty that lies at the heart of things

Joy

Integration of more of myself when I experience the healing power of God at work in my life

A new start—forgiveness

A sense of serving a larger purpose

Awe and wonder

All is well even when it isn't

Being in communion with the Divine Presence

Love!

Thomas Kelly, a Quaker, speaks eloquently about what draws us to God. In his *Testament of Devotion*, one of the great books on practical mysticism in our time, he says:

We Western peoples are apt to think our great problems are external, environmental. We are not skilled in the inner life, where the real roots of our problem lie. . . . The outer distractions of our interests reflect an inner lack of integration of our own lives. We are trying to be several selves at once, without all our selves being organized by a single, mastering Life within us. . . .

And we are unhappy, uneasy, strained, oppressed, and fearful we shall be shallow. For over the margins of life comes a whisper, a faint call, a premonition of richer living which we know we are passing by. Strained by the very mad pace of our daily outer burdens, we are further strained by an inward uneasiness, because we have hints that there is a way of life vastly richer and deeper than all this hurried existence, a life of unhurried serenity and peace and power. If only we could slip over into that Center![1]

Kelly speaks for many of us. We sense that the "premonition of richer living which we know we are passing by" will continue to haunt us because it is the very nature of humanity to settle for nothing less than the life of the spirit. Even for the many in our society who aren't at all sure there is a God, the instinct for deeper meaning is irrepressible. There is a compelling light which continues to appear at the edge of our vision. We see something and we want to see more.

In Peter Beagle's wonderful fantasy, *The Last Unicorn*, a unicorn was on a road, passing a man hoeing his field. The man straightened up when he saw her. "Oh," he said. "Oh, you're beautiful." But then he said, "Pretty . . . you pretty little mare."[2] He thinks she's a horse! He sees but he is sightless. And yet he knows, somewhere deep in himself, that this is more than a horse, and he is drawn to her. That's the story of us all. We are deeply drawn to God. Even when we mistake unicorns for horses, we know there is something "richer and deeper" and we want more of it.

But now comes a searching question: If the encounters with God draw us so deeply and hold so much promise, why aren't we all saints? If the spiritual life is that rich, why don't more of us really go for it? Why don't we trail God night and day until we run God down for good? What holds us back?

When we face into such questions, we come to our first great crossroads in the spiritual journey. We encounter our fears. We find that we not only want more of God in our lives but that we are frightened of the consequences of moving too close. We bump into shadows, often unnamed but present, which haunt our souls. We may try to touch the unicorn but it doesn't take much to scare us away.

In my experience, many people can't move deeper into their spiritual journeys until they look at their worst fantasies of what might happen if they were to get more intentional about making more room for God. Over the years I have seen people wrestle hard with what they imagine are the consequences of becoming too close to God. Over and over again, certain common responses emerge as fears are acknowledged:

God, if there is a God, might let me down—I don't care to put that to the test.

If this means going to the slums of Calcutta with Mother Teresa, I'm not cut out for the life.

I may have to give up everything I enjoy.

This might lead to martyrdom!

I might become so spiritual my family and friends will laugh at me—or leave me.

I'll lose my autonomy.

God will turn out to be a perfectionistic taskmaster.

God may insist that I toil night and day with no time out for fun.

It takes more trust than I've got—in God and in myself.

I resent the idea of surrendering my hard won independence to anyone, including God.

"Religious experience" scares me.

Does this mean I have to go to church every Sunday?

God might want all of me when I'm only willing to give some of me.

I don't want to lose control.

I'm not good enough.

I'll have to change; it's too painful.

I may find that God doesn't exist.

This list speaks for itself. There is little doubt that people are drawn to know God better but there's also little doubt that we are reluctant to go for it. Our fears and worst fantasies are considerable. I've discovered that's just as true for those who are well launched on the spiritual journey as for those who are just starting. It's true for clergy, monks and nuns, and it's true for most religious people, lay or ordained. It's true for people of every religion. Usually it is a great relief to put those feelings on the table and learn that others share them, too.

What then? Are we stuck between our hopes and our fears? Certainly if God is actually like some of our worst fears, it would be foolish for us to draw near and wise for us to keep our distance.

We're not fools.

I have discovered both in myself and with those whom I try to assist in their spiritual growth that there are two steps which help us move through this barrier of fear.

The first step is to undo the false images of God we frequently carry from our childhood. This step is not necessary for everyone because some of us have been fortunate: the Divine Presence has been a friendly presence from the beginning. But for others, much has to be undone. None of us in our right minds will be interested in going further on the spiritual journey if God is seen as an oppressor, an enemy or a terrifying presence who desires nothing but to shape us up with bizarre rules and impossible demands such as are too often taught in some churches or by some families. I remember the story a man told me about his time in a monastery. Placed there by his fervently religious mother and a despotic God and somehow escaping the usual careful screening of the monks, he was admitted to one of the less savory monastic communities of pre-Vatican II days and became a tortured soul. Months passed until somehow, by the grace of the real

God, he left that place and re-entered the world. Understandably he stayed away from all things religious for years. Still, something stirred in him which called him to deeper spiritual health. He sought out a psychotherapist and he looked for a spiritual director. It was when he understood that it was the real God who had called him out of the monastery rather than who had trapped him in it that he slowly began to put the spiritual pieces of his life back together. He understood that the real God is a God of health and wholeness, not of tyranny and oppression. The man had to undo his mother's view of God to find the God of Jesus.

There is a second step we can take if we are to move through our fears. It can be of great help to get in touch with our own best experiences of God. When we do so, we discover there is a great difference between our worst fears of what may happen to us if we go on the spiritual journey and the actual experiences we have had with God. When we remember what God is really like and how good it is to be with God, we take heart. When we recall the texture of our encounters with God and how we felt during and after them, powerful, healing memories are summoned and we can move ahead.

One evening, in a class on the spiritual life, the leaders invited their class to consider a time when each felt that he or she had encountered God, the texture of those encounters and the feelings each had before and afterward. Each class member sat quietly, sometimes thinking, sometimes writing. After a few minutes all were asked to share anything they wished.

Several persons said they felt that they had encountered God in nature—a mountain etched against a sunset had moved one person, while another remembered being "struck dumb" by the sight of the stars when he was nine.

Some believed they had encountered God through other people. One mentioned she had known someone who seemed to be "genuinely authentic, centered in spirit and in mind." Another said he learned about God's closeness and concern through the faith and struggles of friends as they worked through their final days together during a death in the family.

The comments from the group varied. One man felt he encountered God when his son was born; he was aware of a deep sense of order—the inner connectedness and rightness behind things. Someone else spoke about the inner experience of "peace, calmness and strength" that sometimes comes to her in prayer. Another woman mentioned that she frequently felt led by a power beyond her to exactly what she needed; often, after asking for guidance, she came across a sentence or paragraph in a book that seemed just right. One man said he experienced a sense of Sacred Presence especially when he invited God to come into the midst of his doubts, moments of confusion and times of anxiety.

Another man said that meditation had helped him better learn to "let go of the need to hold onto things so tightly." He said that he found he did not have to control things so much as had once been the case. He also noted that he felt "less in need of proving myself in such a compulsive way" and that he was more present to himself and to life. He felt that something "profound and gracious—it must be God in my depths" was working to free him up.

Still another spoke about the simple trust and humility that opens in him when he becomes aware of what happens in the liturgical drama and offering of holy communion when Christ draws so close to a congregation.

A particularly powerful example was shared toward the end of the evening by a man who spoke about his fear that should he pursue the spiritual life, God would make him work endless hours more each week than he already worked. He was worried that "if he became even more open to the spiritual process, God would do him in." He shared this for a while and then his mood shifted. He became reflective and quiet. He was getting in touch with an earlier memory. When he spoke again he said that he had just recalled an experience of a few years back when he had felt especially close to God. He remembered feeling nourished, as though he was in the presence of a Divine Companion who had nothing but his best interests at heart. The man felt so solid and secure during that encounter that he decided to summon his courage and ask God to show him what God had in mind for him. For three days after, he found himself the recipient of all sorts of homely little gifts—a card of appreciation came in the mail for a long forgotten favor, someone invited him to lunch at a restaurant where he had always wanted to eat, an appointment was canceled and he had time to breathe in the middle of a frantic day. Were these coincidences? Perhaps—there was no way to tell for sure—but he also wondered if God might not be responding to his prayer in a simple, direct way.

Whatever might or might not have happened, the man recalled that in the weeks which followed he began to feel differently about God. He realized that he was much harder on himself than God was. He began to see that God was not the same as his father who had expected much more from him than he could possibly manage. Now, in the class, he recalled again what an impact this had on him. He told us that if he could trust his own best experiences of God, he didn't have to stay as stuck in his fear of going further on the spiritual path. A few weeks later, he told me how much had started to come together for him. He realized that while God certainly did have expectations of him they were different than he had imagined. God wanted him to learn to let go of an obsessive pattern to be such a perfect performer in favor of becoming an easier person to live with—both in himself and with his family and business partners. This was indeed a mighty work for him to "perform," but it had a far different quality to it than what he had previously believed God would have expected of him. God was dealing with him much differently and in a much better fashion than he could have dreamed. He felt safe and trusting enough of God to consider the spiritual path more seriously.

After the group had finished sharing, it was clear that there is great range in the ways human beings experience a sense of the Holy. Even though some of the class members were unsure about the exact nature of God, there was a sense shared by most of being rooted in a deep and loving mystery at the core of things.

Again and again people report that such experiences have

a loving character to them. Most report that they experience God as a deep and accepting Presence. They are aware that the Divine Presence leaves them feeling both more at home in life and more challenged to grow. They feel opened up. Most of all they regain their trust. They believe that God will be with them on their journey. This gives them the courage to move ahead.

The journalist Marjorie Holmes has written a book called *How Can I Find You, God?* in which she speaks of the many ways she has experienced God. Her list is extraordinary just because it is full of so many ordinary things. She believes that God generally comes to us not in strange or exotic ways but usually in the stuff of daily living. She has found the Divine Friend "through people, through the wonders of nature, through the bliss of birth and the testing of pain and death, through books and art and work and prayer."[2] Holmes writes of the many avenues God has used to teach her to trust more and to open her soul. She mentions how God used an intelligent and perceptive friend to challenge her assumption that God is just one more hard taskmaster. She speaks of the change she experienced in perspective when her first child began to grow within her. She mentions books by Albert Schweitzer, David Wilkerson, Emmet Fox and especially Brother Lawrence as full of grace for her. She recalls God's presence on a February day when she stretched out on a wooden bench in her yard to gaze up at the trees which, like nude dancers, reached up and out, opening themselves to the sky as if to give and receive, thereby teaching her something about receiving and giving. She tries to imagine the world without music and then sees that something so nourishing and powerful reveals something about the Divine Source itself. She wrestles with the reality of pain and discovers that she has learned something of the suffering love of God through her own suffering love for those in pain.

Holmes puts into words the texture of what many people have experienced in their encounters with the Holy One. They find that this Presence is replete with such grace and fullness that when one becomes aligned with it things have a way of falling into perspective. However that Presence has been experienced—and that happens in ways that are congruent for each individual—the consequences are similar. In the Loving Presence people become more open to the possibility of letting go of old fears and resistances. They discover that those things that cause them to hold back from the spiritual path, while still present and often very powerful, have begun to have less of a death grip.

This chapter began with the muppets drawing away from the secrets of the universe for a mediocre beef stew. So long as people believe the spiritual life carries a double message, that of God's love over against what they suspect might be God's intention to do them in, they are going to remain ambivalent about pursuing the spiritual path. They are going to be on guard. As mediocre as beef stew might be, it is at least a compromise that keeps one going in some fashion. Who wants to swim far in the spiritual ocean if God turns out to be a shark? Or might ask us to swim further out than we want to?

It takes courage to leave the beach and swim out to sea. It is no simple matter. Jesus' disciples discovered that. They followed him and they held back. We can understand. He told them that they would be changed (they would "lose their lives") and he also promised that they would find new life beyond their best dreams, in "good measure, pressed down, shaken together and running over . . ." (Lk 6:38). It would mean they would have to let go of that which was false. It would mean they would have to trust him as much as they could. That trust didn't come easily. Peter struggled with it right up to Christ's crucifixion.

The great spiritual teachers tell us that when the Divine Life is born in us, that which is false and illusory begins to die. This is promising and it is frightening. No one can face that unless he or she is pretty sure that beneath that which is unreal there is a deeper and better reality. When we start to trust our own best experiences of God, the One who says, "Have no fear," and "I am with you always," that deeper reality begins to come forth. Then we can move ahead.

There is a story of a king who went mad and moved to the cellar of his palace. There he sat in the midst of rags and bones which he clung to as his treasures. His advisors urged him to leave, reminding him of all the rooms in the palace that were full of real treasures. The king wouldn't budge. He preferred to live in illusion.

So do most of us until something better comes along.

Like the king's friends, the great spiritual teachers and saints have always tried to awaken the rest of us to the truth that there are glorious and sometimes unknown rooms in our souls. These great souls have never said they are traveling a way meant for a privileged few. They know it is possible for any one of us to experience the incredible reality of God just as they have. They know what it is like to be loved by God so much that nothing else can match that experience and the search to deepen and enlarge it. They know that the spiritual life is a natural human activity that requires not special powers but the willingness to open doors.[4]

How do we open those doors? It happens when we learn to move through our fears of what might happen to us if we become more spiritual, to that place where we begin to trust our best experiences of God—experiences which have helped us see that God is even better than we had hoped.

Frederick Buechner says it beautifully:

We are all of us more mystics than we believe or choose to believe. . . . We have seen more than we let on, even to ourselves. Through some moment of beauty or pain, some sudden turning of our lives, we catch glimmers at least of what the saints are blinded by, only then, unlike the saints, we tend to go on as though nothing has happened. To go on as though something has happened, even though we are not sure what it was or just where we are supposed to go with it, is to enter the dimension of life that religion is a word for.[5]

COMING TO GOD
AS WE ARE

Something vital is born in us when trust takes root. Something from the ground of life stirs in us once we build on our experiences of God enough to consider moving through our resistances and fears. The promise of something better pulls at us. We are ready to move another step. How do we begin?

We begin where we are.

When trust for God begins to be formed in us, a vital discovery takes place when we realize that we can approach God as we are, not as we imagine we are supposed to be. This sounds so easy. It usually is not. Even if our theology teaches us that God loves us, a great many of us believe that we can only come to God as we should be. We doubt that we are accepted if we appear as we really are.

If we don't live out of our own center, we live out of something or someone else's center. If we try to live from out of anything less than ourselves, we can't get far in the spiritual life because we pass before the face of the Divine One like strangers. We bring nothing genuine for God to love, and there is nothing authentic we present for transformation. If we are unwilling to reveal ourselves as we are to God or even to ourselves, we remain hollow.

For many it is difficult to believe that we don't have to be someone else or somewhere else such as off in the future when we will be "more perfect" than now.

In the classes on spiritual growth which we teach at the Center for Spiritual Development, members are asked to get into this issue by writing private letters to God which share whatever they want to say about themselves and about God, especially about what they need, or would like, or about which they are concerned. Some have no trouble with this.

Some do because they aren't convinced it's possible to speak to God until they are more perfect. Here are a few examples:

> I can't talk to God until I am calm or loving.
>
> I can't talk to God because I haven't prayed for a long time.
>
> I can't talk to God because I have sexual feelings.
>
> I can't talk to God because I have doubts.
>
> I can't talk to God until my life is in order.

There are many variations on the same theme that we can't come to God until we are "good enough." Even when we have been taught to believe differently—that God loves us—it is hard to soak that fundamental reality fully up into our pores. It is not always easy to imagine that we can truly be ourselves before God.

Shelia, a sixty year old woman, who by her own definition has "learned wisdom the long-way around," has shared her difficulty about what it means to come to God as a real human being. From her youth she had been programmed by her family and her church to be a "model woman." Because she was bright and attractive, she pulled off what she imagined this to be very well. In high school she had been a cheerleader and an officer of the student body. In college she joined practically every organization on campus and provided an empathetic ear for anyone who needed to talk. After graduation and a short-term stint with a Chicago retail store, she married, began her family and settled into a life of middle-class comforts with its expected values of family, church, clubs, and volunteer work. For many years life seemed full to her.

About the time Shelia's second of three children left the nest, she had two profound shocks. Her husband had an affair and her oldest child tried to commit suicide. Her life of fabricated meaning started to unravel. Shelia, who had been the envy of her friends and the mainstay of her church and several important volunteer organizations, ran into a wall. She found that she had been filling the role of perfect wife and mother, playing out the expectations that had been drilled into her from early childhood by everyone including herself. Deep inside, she had known things weren't going as well as she had pretended but she couldn't admit it and had refused to enter into the problems of her marriage or her children. She had kept herself bright and busy, even in her prayers, to protect herself from the pain and from her sense of fear and inadequacy.

In agony, Shelia began to re-examine her life and her shaky value system. For three years she visited a psychotherapist, finding counseling an immensely supportive way to take stock of her broken life. She also began to rework her sense of God. As she began to open the windows and doors of her inner life, she realized how much, over the years, God had become for her little more than a cosmic superperson who wanted her to be just like God. Shelia began to pray with new intensity, inviting God to deal with her as she was. She told God she was tired of pretending, and she began to face into her own needs with new compassion. "Even though I had heard again and again in church that God loves us as we are and not just for what we do, I finally began to learn for myself that this is really true," she said. Very slowly she began to get in touch with her anger. For years she had tried to meet other people's expectations, trying to keep things harmonious, making herself available to all. Now she saw how unauthentic this was. As her real feelings emerged, she became more and more of her own person, not as worried about letting others be responsible for their own lives. It was, she said, like a springtime thaw after a long, hard winter. Something more authentic was coming to life, and what God had in mind for her began to be seen as much better than Shelia had been able to imagine.

John Powell, a Jesuit priest, who has wrestled with his own problems in being himself before God, writes what it has meant to come to God as he is, not as he believed he should be:

Speaking to God honestly is the beginning of prayer; it locates a person before God. . . . Without such self-disclosure there is no real giving, for it is only in that moment when we are willing to put our true selves on the line, to be taken for better or worse, to be accepted or to be rejected, that true interpersonal encounter begins . . . for love demands presence, not presents. All my gifts (presents) are mere motion until I have given my true self (presence) in honest self revelation.

As in all interpersonal relationships, so in the relationship with God. I do not put myself into his hands or confront his freedom of choice to accept me or reject me, to love me or to loathe me, until I have told him who I am. Only then can I ask him: Will you have me? Will you let me be yours? Will you be mine? Martin Luther's first law of successful prayer is: Don't lie to God! . . . In speaking to God . . . we must reveal our true and naked selves. We must tell him the truth of ourselves. We must tell him the truth of our thoughts, desires and feelings, whatever they may be. They may not be what I would like them to be, but they are not right or wrong, true or false. They are me.[1]

Besides finding it difficult to come to God because they don't feel worthy, some people are blocked because they believe that since God knows what they think and feel in the first place, it is a waste of time to take up God's time or theirs. Why bother?

If we truly have a relationship with God and God truly cares about us, reality is much richer than this. A relationship by nature involves mutual respect and freedom. No relationship worth its salt can be forced or coerced. Our freedom is so precious to God that it won't be violated even if God knows what is best for us. God waits for us to take our part in the relationship. God waits for us to speak, to ask, to share. That speaking, asking and sharing are essential ingredients in our growth. We are invited to take part in the process of becoming mature sons and daughters of the Divine Parent. God gives us many blessings before we ask, but one of God's greatest blessings is that of waiting for us to assume our part in shaping who we are and what we want to be.

The Heavenly One knows what we need before we ask. God knows what is on our hearts and minds before we speak. But God will not enter the inner door of our lives until we take hold for ourselves of what it is that we need. Such speaking and sharing is a sign that we are willing to exercise our capacity for spiritual development. God is with us long before we speak, and is with us in our very speaking, but God will not shape our words or our feelings for us; that is our privilege. Then, after our speaking, God responds—either in some direct fashion or more indirectly by waiting until we learn to speak in ways that are more closely attuned to God's loving will for us.

Many people have no particular trouble believing that it is possible to speak to the Divine One or that God hears them, but they are not sure they can get through. They feel that between God's holiness and their humanity a great gulf is fixed. There are, they believe, two separate worlds, "spiritual" and "real." Only in special moments of purity can the chasm be bridged.

Bill is a middle-aged man who used to believe he could only come to God if the conditions were just right—both in his own life and in the physical environment. As a teenager he had attended a summer camp in the mountains. The natural beauty of that camp had kindled a sense of God's presence within him, as had the hymns and stories around the campfire which had encouraged him to "give himself to God." This he did, but soon afterward, when he returned home, he experienced guilt and despair when his parents were divorced. For many years thereafter, he could only feel close to God when the conditions were right, especially only in the mountains or if he felt "pure" enough.

A crisis in Bill's own marriage and a subsequent separation changed his point of view. The loneliness he was experiencing compelled him to share his feelings with a business partner. He was so moved by the sensitive response and continuing help of his colleague, a deeply spiritual person who himself had recently been divorced, that Bill began to question the split he had placed between the God he had experienced in the mountains and the rest of his life. Over a period of weeks he began to believe that God wasn't limited to mountains or elevated feelings around the campfire. Bill believed that God had been particularly close in the quiet, steadying presence of his friend. He began to think that, like his friend, he could approach God when he was in pain and need as well as in "mountaintop" experiences. It was as though a closed-off part of himself opened up. He began to see that it was not in God's nature to be present only in rarified and special moments of "perfection." God is present everywhere. Bill started to understand how much more open God had been over the years to him than he had been to God.

When we launch forth on the spiritual journey there is only one place we can begin, and that is with ourselves before a God who takes us where we are.

Probably no one has written more compellingly about the importance of coming to God with one's full humanity than has Archbishop Anthony Bloom. He says that a great many books on prayer make him uneasy because they act as though both God and the person who is praying to God are hardly present. He reminds us that the gospel tells us that the kingdom of God is within us. If we can't meet God there, in the depth of ourselves, our chances of meeting the Beloved One anywhere else are pretty remote. Therefore, the first act of prayer is to choose such words as are "completely true to what you are, words which you are not ashamed of, which express you adequately. . . ."[2] In other words, whatever we do with God, first of all we need to be honestly and fully involved in mind and heart.

The first thing which I suggest, therefore, is that you should ask yourself what words of prayer make sense for you to offer to God, whether they be your own or those of other people. Ask yourself also how much they touch your heart, to what extent you are capable of concentrating your mind on them—for if you cannot be attentive to the words you say, why should God? How can He receive them as an expression of love if you do not put your heart into them, if you have only put in a certain amount of courtesy together with a certain amount of absent-mindedness?[3]

The place to start with the spiritual journey, when with the help of trust we move beyond our stuck places, is with ourselves before a God who takes us where and as we are. There is no other place to begin. We are who we are. We are no less and no more farther along the path than at this moment. This is great "good news." We can come as we are in the midst of our joys and our sorrows, with the strengths that are in fact ours and with the warts that cover us. We tell the Divine One who we are and who we aren't. We become more honest about our belief and our unbelief. We sing out our delight in exclamations of awe and through quiet words of profound thanksgiving. We express our resentments at what seem to us to be times when we are taken for granted and when we feel misused. Sometimes neurotically, sometimes with health, we tell the truth as we see it.

When we come with attentiveness to ourselves as we really are, we make friends with God. In making friends with God, we also make friends with ourselves, for we find that while we have hidden from ourselves and the universe like shy creatures which have concealed themselves until they learn they won't be harmed, we find with God that we are increasingly able to emerge from our hiding places. We begin to stand forth. Embraced by God, we learn to embrace ourselves moment by moment and step by step. Real life begins. The spiritual journey is underway.

LISTENING

If one of the first steps in the spiritual life involves putting ourselves on the line with God the way we are, the next step involves listening to God. A relationship is always a two way street.

No matter how honest we are about who we are, if we aren't also open to receiving what God has to say in return, we haven't closed the circle. We have insisted on maintaining control. A relationship with the Holy One can't be very profound if we are only willing to tell God what we have to say but aren't willing to hear what God has to say to us as well. There is a shift here from us to God. There needs to be a conversion—a moving beyond the good things that happen to us when we become more honest to the good things that happen when the Spirit becomes an end in her own right—when we welcome the Spirit for her own sake and for what she has to teach us. It's a good thing in any relationship, human or divine, to express oneself in a more genuine way to another, and it's a further thing to become more transparent to the other as well. Then control is lessened. Relationship is enhanced.

If we are to listen for God, we need to find out how God speaks to us. Is it in "religious language," in "thee's and 'thou's"? Is it in the language of a favorite version of the Bible or a sanctified version of a prayer book? Does God speak only when we are good enough? Does God speak only to Christians or only to Jews or only to Muslims or Hindus or Buddhists? Does God use a voice or speak only through miracles?

I believe that God speaks in ways that are meaningful to us. I believe God speaks and acts in ways that are congruent with our natures and in touch with our temperaments. This doesn't mean that God is limited to our ability to hear. The Gracious One is revealed in ways that stretch us beyond ourselves and our boundaries, as, for example, the cradle and cross of Christ which jolted people as being ill-suited to the ways they imagined God would do things. Still, God comes to us and speaks in ways that touch who we are as we are. Any other way of speaking would be less than loving and quite impossible anyway. No matter what it is that is said, even from the highest level of understanding, how can one speak to another except as one speaks so the other can hear?

Judith, a member of a spiritual growth group, shared with the group members the fact that for several years she had been indignant when the children of her parish came out of Sunday school and into the church service following the sermon for the balance of the parish eucharist. She found the children noisy and disruptive and made no secret of her feelings that they belonged somewhere else.

A few weeks passed following the time that Judith shared her feelings with the group. The group discussion turned to what it meant to offer real life to God; they were learning to talk to God as they were rather than as they should be. Following one of the sessions, it occurred to Judith to tell God about her rancor regarding young children in church. She told God how she felt. She also said she wasn't sure she was going to change her mind but she would like to learn to like children better than she did. She asked God what, if anything, God could do about it if she were open to divine help and willing to listen to what God might have to say.

During the week that followed, she found herself reflecting about her life. She began to feel that she was a self-centered person. It was not that she felt she had to approve of noisy children or even of children in church; many people agreed with her. But in her case she began to feel that most of the things she did revolved around little else than her own whims. And so far as children were concerned she realized she had seldom looked at them except as irritants.

Not long after her self-inventory, Judith was driving by the children's hospital in her city and found herself starting to imagine the sorts of things that took place there. Over the next few days, as she drove past the hospital, something kept prompting her to remember what it was that she knew of the volunteer programs. One day, and with some discomfort, she entered the hospital and asked to speak to the director of volunteers, telling her that she wanted to meet a child. She was sent to a boy in a wheelchair, his arms and legs wizened, his speech so badly impaired that Judith could hardly understand him. She didn't particularly like him but she made an effort to listen to him for a moment or two. This woman, who had usually been impatient and seldom enjoyed listening to anyone, found herself trying to sort out the words of a little boy whom almost no one could understand. It was very difficult. Only a puritanical kind of duty took her back for a second visit. The third visit was different. As she entered his room, the child lifted up his arms and gave her a great hug. She was touched beyond words. Something in her opened up.

Some weeks later Judith shared her experience with the spiritual growth group. She hesitated, not sure that anyone would be interested. The group listened in profound silence. They were deeply moved, aware of how practical and relevant God's answer to Judith had been. She had managed to offer her special frustrations and needs to God, and God had opened a door that was exactly right for her. Later, someone asked her how it was for her in church with the children. She grinned and said that she still didn't especially like it but, to tell the truth, she hadn't thought about it all that much lately.

How does God speak to us? In ways that fit who we are. Judith wanted to learn how to be more loving with children, and God gave her a very practical way to grow in the direction she wanted to grow. It couldn't have been easy for her to speak to the director of volunteers, and it was difficult for her to go back more than once to her little patient. On her part some persistence was required. It was worth it. Beneath the hard crust, something tender opened in her that was more truly who she was and wanted to be. As Judith discovered, when tenderness moves in us we begin to appreciate the world around us. We can't help opening ourselves to what is there beyond us. That is what happened to Judith. She started responding to people and events from her heart. That was what Judith really yearned for, and it was what God was doing in her. She had to ask for help and be willing to receive it. When it came, it was exactly right for her, even better than she could have imagined.

This is typical of God. When God speaks and acts, it is always done in a way that is right for us, that builds us up into more complete versions of who we really are. God's way is to call us to become more congruent with our deepest selves.

What God does and says is right for us as unique individuals. Sometimes we forget that by confusing essence and form. The essence of Judith's spiritual growth was her willingness to be open to God, to take stock and to let God help her. The form was the context in which that growth took place and the shape it took, that is, working with a child at a hospital. Too often we lay the form that is right for one person on another. This might happen when someone, having heard another person complain about noisy children, eagerly greets the complainer with great enthusiasm while telling her, "I know just what you need! You need to start thinking more about others. Have you ever considered volunteering at a children's hospital?"

God addresses each of us by our own names, not by another's. Jesus' destiny led him to the cross. That was, as we know, a struggle for him and he wrestled mightily with it in the Garden of Gethsemane but it was right for him and his life's purpose. He knew that and, as things were resolved in him, he embraced it. There is even a legend that he went to the cross with profound joy in his heart. Will God lead us to a cross? For most of us, probably not. What God will do is lead us to what is right for us and for what it is we are to do in the world. God speaks to and works with us as we are, where we are, as we can hear God and as we are willing to be open to the best that is in us.

Every time I am privileged to be with people as they wrestle with God's will for their lives, this truth comes home to me that there is complete consistency between who we are and what God wants for us. I see again and again how hard it is to believe that it can be this good. I also see what a powerful thing it is when people discover for themselves that doing God's will is tied into being authentically who they are.

In our classes at the Center for Spiritual Development, we often take people through a four step process in learning how to discern God's will. The first step involves getting in touch with a decision they are wrestling with. The second is to become conscious of the voices from their past which are influencing them, consciously or unconsciously about that decision, such as parental figures, pastors, teachers, or anyone else with authority in their lives. The third step is to become better acquainted with their own deepest desires in the matter they are considering. The fourth step is to ask what God's will is. This is a revealing exercise for most people. They find that they often equate the second step, voices from their authority figures, with the fourth step, the will of God. Many also find it very difficult to get in touch with the third step, their own deepest and best desires. Even more, they can't imagine that God's will and their own deepest and best desires have anything to do with each other.

If we believe that God's will is fixed on an immutable stone tablet totally independent of our inner selves, we miss a deeper truth, namely, that God's will is best found in us, congruent with our deepest selves and our deepest truths and desires. This doesn't mean that God's will is to be equated with our whims or fancies, nor does it mean that we don't look beyond ourselves for revelation, assistance and wisdom. It does mean that to find God's will, we must go to those places within that reveal who we most truly are and what we most truly need.

Sister Katherine Dyckman and Father Patrick Carroll have illustrated what this can mean:

> Beneath the question of human motivation lies the reoccuring query: "How does one find God's will?" . . . It makes a great deal of difference, obviously, whether our

framework places God's will outside ourselves, pre-determined, written on some eternal scroll, or whether that will is inside, coincidental with our deepest desires. We believe that we discover the will of God within ourselves. . . . When we most clearly know ourselves, we best know where and how God speaks to us.

A priest ordained five years, loving the ministry, but finding constant tension in the style of life that priesthood includes (celibate, all male community, living in the same place one works, twenty-four hours a day on call, etc.) searches to discover God's will for him in his future. Can he stay as a priest and not die as a person? Is it possible for him to move elsewhere and still be faithful to God? . . . If God's will is external to him along with all that he has experienced, all he is feeling and hoping for the future, then this will is immutable and determined. His decision must be to remain where he is. If God's will is discovered deeply within himself as he reflects on the importance of the choices he has made, his need to be faithful to relationships he has built up as a priest, his love of ministry, and his continued ability to feel and be alive and life-giving to others, he may be led to a new choice, with this new evidence, and a much clearer picture of what the deepest self in him really wants.

God's will is not found in our doing whatever we want, acting on whim. God does not baptize our silly frivolous choices (though he does still love us). But we believe God's will is found in doing what we want at the very best and deepest level of who we understand ourselves to be. This is quite different.[1]

In other words, listening to God means understanding that being authentically oneself and being who God wants one to be are the same thing. Learning to become God's person is involved with becoming more empowered from within.

John Powell believes that if speaking to God is no simple matter, listening is no simple matter either. He wonders, as we all do, how God communicates with us. If we have some sense of that we shall be more able to recognize what God sounds like and better listen for God's voice.

It may take some training to learn to tune into God, meditation as we shall see in a later chapter being one means to sensitize ourselves, but there is no great mystery, Powell says, in the channels God uses to get through to us. God speaks through the channels of our minds, wills, emotions, imaginations and memories—in other words through the familiar faculties of perception.

Powell's description of how God speaks through his mind is a good example. It summarizes the experience of many people, including my own:

> After putting myself before the Lord, he comes to me to help me see the person, the problems I have described through his eyes and in his eternal perspective. He puts his ideas into my mind, and especially his perspectives. He widens my vision, helps me to see what is really important in life and to distinguish the really important from the unimportant. I have always wanted to define delusion as the confusion of what is important in life with the unimportant. I personally get up-tight, blow things up out of all proportion, especially when the lightning strikes close to the home of my ego. I enter the wrong arenas to do battle, focus on the wrong issues of contention. And I tell him all about it. Then he comes, and, in his own gentle way, fills my mind with his thoughts and his vision. He undeludes me.[2]

Some people wonder if it is God speaking or just their own auto-suggestion. We need to be modest; we're quite capable of fooling ourselves. But there is another question that needs to be asked, too. Just because we can fool ourselves, does that automatically prevent God from having access to us? Healthy skepticism has its place, but too much of it can block us from becoming attuned to the quiet wisdom of God which is much more available than we often imagine to guide and direct us.

It has been my experience that the reason many of us

have difficulty in believing that God can speak to us has less to do with healthy skepticism than it has to do with fear and self-doubt. We doubt that God really wants to speak to us and we are afraid that God might! It is one thing to believe that the Divine One may reach into the lives of others, especially great spiritual teachers, but it is another thing to believe that God will come to us as well.

The Bible is a great help here! The men and women of the Bible are not generally realized spiritual masters. They are very human people who are extraordinary only in the sense that they find the courage and faith to make themselves accessible to God. Moses, having fled to the desert to raise sheep for his father-in-law, was quite human in his resistance to God's summons to return to Egypt to free the Hebrew slaves; he didn't want to go! What was extraordinary about him is that he did listen to God's promptings; he did go. Jeremiah told God to get off his back because he was too young to be a prophet. Still, when God promised to be with him and touched his lips with authority, Jeremiah went before the powerful and spoke. Peter, in great fear, pulled back hard the night before Jesus was crucified, but after the resurrection he became a spiritual dynamo.

We all pull back. We do that for fear and we do it because we wonder how it is that God would come to people like us in the first place. Who are we after all? What kind of God would come to someone so unworthy and unimportant as I am? Groucho Marx is supposed to have said: "I wouldn't belong to a club that would take in someone like me!"

To deal with that kind of question we have to move beyond our self-centeredness, disguised as self-abnegation. There is true humility and there is pseudo-humility. God has better things to say about us than we have to say about ourselves. It is God's desire to speak to us. It is God's delight to fill us with God's own life, to find a home in our minds, wills, hearts, imaginations and bodies. It is God's infinite pleasure to indwell us and to invite us into deeper union. Are we willing to hear that?

It's a big step for many people to feel that the Infinite

Spirit actually wishes to live and move and express itself in us. It's not easy to remember, especially in our bad days or when the world looks bleak, that we are to be songs of the Divine Singer. Maybe that's what's hard about listening. When we listen, we begin to see that we have to become open to what someone is saying to and about us. If we really listen, we make room to be perceived! Few of us care to be perceived all that much. Who knows what warts may stand forth? Or who knows what love may come through? Surprisingly, not all of us are sure we want to be loved that much. We all yearn to be truly loved but, perhaps because we have been hurt and fear being hurt again or because we are frightened of the claims to grow which love puts to us, we often find it easier to put ourselves down than open ourselves to those positive messages of love and their challenge to become whole. Still, the loving messages from God keep coming. What then? We can choose not to listen, but this is to refuse to grow. How long shall we continue to blame the hurts that have come to us in the past for our refusal to hear good tidings in the present? Our ability to listen to the Spirit is directly related to how we choose to assume responsibility for the way we accept or discount the messages of Divine Love that keep coming our way.

A man had a dream in which he saw himself before God. The dream began with him experiencing himself as a worthless speck before the feet of the Divine Presence. Then a voice addressed him: "This is not how I see you; it is how you see yourself. I love you!"

Will God speak to us and come to us? A more searching question is: Do we want God to speak to us and come to us? Are we willing to be open to something as powerful as God's loving messages?

Listening happens when we make room for the Spirit to address us. Listening means opening ourselves up to One who will empower and transform and love us into more than we can imagine. The ultimate in listening is when we make room for God to take command of our lives and move us toward better things.

GROWTH

Somewhere in her writings Evelyn Underhill likens the spiritual journey to a climb in the Alps. It begins on the veranda of a mountain hotel where a glimpse is caught of a magnificent peak. Some people are drawn further. They decide to climb. At first the path leads through flower meadows, but after a time the climbers find themselves in boulder fields and the real work begins.

What I have talked about so far in this book is like the first steps up the mountain, from veranda out onto the path to the peak. We have seen the mountain and have been drawn to it. We have imagined the worst and resisted, but finally, trusting our own best experiences of other walks, we have decided to proceed. As we climb we find ourselves learning to let go of some of our baggage by coming to God as we are. And we are beginning to listen to the sounds of divine life all around us as we move upward in the silent mountain air.

We also bump into ourselves. Some things are going to have to change if we are to move on. We need to be in training, we need a guide, we need to unload the many things that hinder our climb. It is a time of purification and inner growth.

How does inner growth take place? How does one move into the different stages of the spiritual life? Sad to say, there has too often been an absence of meaningful assistance.

Liberal Christianity has frequently implied that growth is something one can accomplish through rational thought as though change is rather easy and that what is required is simply to call the need for it to our attention. If people are not being loving enough, what is called for is exhortation to love better. We can deal with our darkness by preaching or educating it away.

Fundamentalism has frequently implied that change is

impossible through rational processes alone—that people need something more profound than exhortation. However, the emphasis is also often on a quick cure, the born-again experience, rather than on a continuing search for still deeper truth. Truth is sometimes defined in terms of being "in" or "out"—in the grace of God or out of the grace of God—with little attention to "sanctification"—the long term integration and growth about which the contemplatives and mystics of the church have so much to say.

For growth to be possible, it is necessary to see ourselves both realistically and optimistically. If we are to be realistic about human nature, we know it does us no good to underestimate the task. St. Paul's realism in the epistle to the Romans, "For even though the desire to do good is in me, I am not able to do it. I don't do the good I want to do" (Rom 7:18–19), finds a contemporary echo in psychoanalysis:

> But competent psychoanalysts still do not underestimate the persistent power of the irrational in shaping and limiting human lives, and they therefore remain skeptical of the quick cure, the deceptively easy answer, the trendy or sensationalistic.[1]

Optimistically, we need to know that we are always in the grace of God. No matter how tangled we are, there is no way we can get out of God's love, God's desire to help us, or the ingrown drive God has planted in us for health and ever deepening truth. That drive exists in the "saved" and the "damned" alike and can never be totally covered over. I believe that it is one of the signs of God's presence in each of God's children.

If our spiritual journey doesn't include both realism and optimism it can't take us far if we really intend to grow. A too optimistic spirituality that works only with the conscious processes will have little lasting impact on us both because it is naive about human nature and the need for grace, and because it has little power to promote creativity. Creativity is dependent upon access to the unconscious process, and a person cut off from his or her unconscious is severely handicapped. On the other hand, an unduly pessimistic spirituality can have a negative and damaging impact. It can minimize, censor and split-off the vehicle for grace—the human personality and body—thereby repressing that which makes us fully human and beloved children of a loving God.

How can we change?

It is no simple, matter. We can't just be exhorted to change. Nor is it a magical, instant fix. Though God is as close to us now as God ever will be in the future, the journey into a closer life with the Gracious One is a long one. It takes continuing courage and a lot of support. Indeed, the more spiritual a person is, the more courage it takes to grow and to seek help while growing. This is totally different than the popular idea that when we become more spiritual, we outgrow the need for help.

To be open to growth takes courage. It begins by finding the courage to believe that change is even possible. It's a good thing we have others to show us the way, because without them we might settle for Hollywood and Madison Avenue as our icons of human destiny. One of the saddest commentaries on our time is that we have almost lost our genuine heroes and heroines. This is even sadder in the church because most Christians don't even know who their saints are or that they are far more than stained glass figures. Fortunately, the truth is far better; the saints are flesh and blood people. They discover God through their humanity. It does a disservice to put them on pedestals because they were never there. They are tempted as are we all and often as tangled. They also know what the grace of God can do in a person's life. Mother Teresa, when asked by a reporter how she felt about being called a living saint, was quite unabashed. "We're meant to be holy," she told him, "you in your job as a reporter and me in mine. To be holy is to be fully alive."

It takes courage to believe that kind of growth into God is not only possible for other people but for oneself. When we face into this reality we confront the truth about ourselves. Our fears come to the surface. The health that is in us battles our desire to run away. These are some of life's most important moments. There is no assurance of what we shall choose. We may move ahead, we may not. It is just at these points we move toward the divine peak or turn back to the veranda.

How can we move ahead? An important step can be taken, as I tried to say in the chapter entitled "What Draws Us to God?/What Holds Us Back?," when we learn to trust our own best experiences as signposts of reality and then, in moments of deep courage, act on them. It is like turning on the light switch in a dark room. We have seen the light in those rooms which are the lives of other people, and so we know it is possible to change things. We remember the times in our own lives when our own rooms have been full of light. In a moment of courage, we reach out to turn the switch.

Moments of truth come upon us again and again to act upon our best experiences of reality.

When I grew up in Denver, the most important sport among my high school friends was skiing. Because their friendship was important to me, I went skiing with them every Saturday, but the only part I enjoyed was the train ride to and from Winter Park. I hated the skiing. It terrified me, and at best, with beating heart, I learned to stem-turn on my long post-World War II wooden skiis on the intermediate slopes. Still, there was one day when it all came together and for a few moments I executed some beautiful parallel turns without falling down. I never forgot how that felt.

Years later, in my forties and living in the Pacific Northwest, I, who had not skied since I was seventeen, looked at the Cascade Mountains to the east of Seattle, and decided I would face into my fear. It was a terrible moment. I didn't in the least want to learn how to ski again, and yet something in me wanted to lean through my fear to something better on the other side. Besides, I remembered how good it felt to do graceful parallel turns. Without inviting anyone, I headed for the hills and signed up for a short ski course. My heart pounded as I put on my rented boots and stepped into my rented skis. All I had to hold me up was my memory of those few wonderful moments years ago. Somehow that memory gave me the courage to proceed. Much to my delight, I did learn to ski—not awfully well but enough to enjoy it for the first time.

I believe this was a spiritual experience. I learned something about trusting myself to life and to my best experiences. It was one of those moments that taught me something about moving into my fears without letting them defeat me. Sometimes I move through them, sometimes I get stuck, but I know what it feels like to move ahead with that fundamental courage for life which I believe has been placed in us by God.

Because God's Spirit has been planted in us, we need to be very clear about something: in spite of our laziness and our outright stubbornness, there are deep resources to help us face into our problems and our fears, and grow. Life's biggest problems generally come when we try to avoid pain, not face it. We do ourselves a great disservice if we try to protect ourselves too much. Something powerful grows in us when we learn to welcome our problems and our resistance points as opportunities for growth rather than as things from which to run. We find God's grace is just as available to the dark corners of our being as to the easy and pleasant places. Nothing is beyond the pale; God can work with anything!

How can we move into our problems rather than away from them?

We need support.

I can't think of that many times in my life when I have been able to make a deep move toward inner health without assistance. My disorders cling to me like vines, choking off my life. I try to improve things and sometimes I can, but I also sometimes get in my own way and step all over myself and others. It's usually when I open myself to empathetic help which empowers me with love, wisdom and confidence that I grow the most. This happens for me through other people and it happens for me with God.

As far as I can see, the most important requirement needed to change besides courage is confidence that God supports us and guides us, confidence that God loves us and believes in us, confidence that God is closer to us than even the worst problems that threaten to undo us. When I open myself to that reality, take it within me and make it part of myself, I can change.

Imagine a person huddled in a cave whose entrance is blocked by a boulder. Outside the sun is warm and the cave-dweller wonders how he can move the boulder to warm himself in the light. Often we think the spiritual life is like that. We imagine that we are alone in our caves, blocked from God by the large boulder of our problems. We believe we have to do everything by ourselves, knocking down our boulders strictly by our own efforts. If we know ourselves well, we despair because we know how heavy the boulders can be.

We don't have to move the boulder all by ourselves.

If we are willing, we can invite God into the cave with us.

If we are willing, we can experience how it is to have God's company in that little space.

If we are willing, we can tell God how things are for us.

In the presence of God, we can see what we are willing to do about our boulders.

There are many things that can happen if we make room for God to join us. Perhaps, feeling less alone, room is made in us for new inspiration and new solutions. Perhaps courage is found to move ahead. Perhaps things fall into perspective. Perhaps we act or we learn to wait for better timing to act.

Perhaps things occur which begin to unblock our emotional lives. What can happen in the presence of God is the softening up of our emotional blocks and strong resistances which have held us captive for so long. As God becomes increasingly real for us—increasingly more of a living presence and increasingly less of a theological concept—we find that we are no longer so identified with those compulsions which had previously seemed so dominant. We begin to find that our identity runs deeper. We begin to become more aware that we have roots in God. We are increasingly alive to the fact that our spirits are dwelling places of something more than even our emotions or our thoughts. An independent, deeper reality grows within us. The Divine Life is coming to life in us. We are still the same people. We carry in us the same old problems. But somehow they have less power. We are grounded in a deeper homeland which, at first, is barely discernible but which, after time, becomes more and more real. We find we are gradually letting go of things to which we had been clinging so tightly. This is God's psychotherapy. As we begin to transfer our attention to God, finding ourselves loved and accepted by that trustworthy presence, we live from a fuller place. We take God into ourselves and learn what it is like to live by a power far better than those influences which had previously seemed so dominant.

We also find that we can look at the dark side of our personalities with more frankness. We find we aren't nearly as well-intentioned as we had imagined. In the pure light of God, which we are beginning to experience more clearly than ever, we see how many shadows there are. This is hardly pleasant. But we find that we are less interested in how pleasant things are than how true they are. If these things exist in us, they exist and we look to God for mercy and for help to let better things come to life. There can be pain in self-recognition but it becomes even more painful to hide from it. If there was nothing there for us but the pain, few of us could face it. Because there is something better, it can be dealt with, even with humor. When we begin to laugh at ourselves, health is just on the other side of the hill!

Jesus tells us where we can find help for growing and changing:

I am the vine, and you are the branches. Whoever remains in me and I in him, will bear much fruit, for you can do nothing without me (Jn 15:5).

He is saying that we cannot develop if we separate ourselves from the greater reality which is God. If we isolate ourselves from that reality of which we are parts, we are branches without nourishment from the vine. Or, as Donald Waters says, we are like guitar strings which are stretched tight but not attached to the instrument's sounding board. Self-preoccupied, we become brittle and thin. To grow, we need to expand. We need to attune and open ourselves to a larger life. We need to reconnect to the Divine Vine that gives rootedness and vitality to everything that is.

There are many ways to become open to our Divine Source so that we may be healed. There is life itself. Clearly the Divine Mystery can touch us in people, in nature, in music, in art. There is also psychotherapy which in my experience has been a powerful way to become more open to the loving movements of divine grace as God seeks to make us whole. As a spiritual director I often recommend it for those who come to me to complement what goes on in spiritual formation. I also believe that most spiritual directors can be of more assistance if they have been in therapy themselves.

There are also the spiritual disciplines which have at their best, over the centuries, provided ways to be in touch with the healing presence of God. These disciplines, such as prayer and fasting, exist not as techniques per se, but as ways to reconnect to the Divine Vine. Among the greatest of those disciplines is meditation, which I will discuss in a later chapter.

Whatever spiritual disciplines we undertake, they are no band aid. The heavy and stubborn patterns which overlay our souls don't magically go away. Spiritual practice is essential, not for its own sake, but to link us up to God and to God's health which lives at the center of each of us. There is no way we can get out of God's love or away from that deep-seated health. We have resources available to us that are mightier than all the powers of the world, even that in us which is resistant to the light and the best interests of our own souls. What is needful is not perfect spiritual practice but our *willingness* to let God's gift of deep health come out of its hiding place and become the operative principle of our lives. That takes courage, but as it rises within us, we find that it's worth more than all the gold of King Midas. We become stronger, clearer and more energized for the journey to the peaks. We become more ourselves than we ever were.

At the heart of the process of reconnecting to the Divine Vine is attunement, which I talk about in the next chapter. The essence of spiritual development is steadily growing receptivity to God's presence through deep love for the Lord.

‖ ATTUNEMENT

Who am I? Probably no culture has made it harder to address that ancient question than ours. At least in most earlier centuries, people knew with whom and to whom they belonged. Even the peasants of medieval Europe, for all their numbing poverty and misery, felt at home in the universe. People these days live on the surface of life, running from fad to fad, because nothing seems enduring or certain enough to hold their attention.

How we yearn to find our identity in something that is rooted in the eternal. How we'd like to move deeper than the surface, beyond our vague groping and further than the boredom and alienation that stem from lack of self. This is our continuing quest; it's at the heart of being human beings. Still, there is a danger. So important is our need for roots that we sometimes give way to fear, turning off our minds or our hearts. History is full of stories of people who have sold out to religious or political fascism in their search for spiritual identity.

The test of any individual and any culture is how deeply and well it attunes itself to the highest influence it knows. At their best the ancient Romans were attuned to a spirit of discipline and patriotism. At their worst they fell in with the cruel games in the Coliseum and lost their souls. At our best in contemporary America we are attuned to a spirit of warm generosity and openness of spirit that makes room for great diversity and welcomes the best efforts of all citizens to better themselves. At our worst our attunement is wolfish; when that spirit prevails there is a giving-over to corrosive envy and to pluralism gone mad so that each part of the larger whole undertakes only its own gain.

We shall never be ourselves until we know we are here to become more and more attuned to something bigger and grander than we are. Nothing less than such attunement will pull out of us that which lies waiting to be completed in us. Until we are turned on to a larger reality, we are like television sets sitting blankly in a room. Until it is plugged in, the set has no purpose; it can only reflect the external play of events on the surface of its picture tube.

Like that television set, we discover that if we are to produce pictures we have to be tuned in to the light that God sends into our darkness. By ourselves we can't make pictures. We can attune ourselves to the power source. Then we can act as transformers of the energy that comes through us. We're deluded if we think we are the source of energy ourselves.

Ours is a great century for believing that humankind can pull its self up by its own spiritual bootstraps. It's not true. I've seen earnest, sincere people who are seriously trying to make spiritual progress hit the wall again and again because they believe the spiritual life equates with turning themselves into perfect people. Donald Walters once pointed out, as I recall, that it takes people a long time to discover that struggling on their own can't take them out of the parameters they have already created, any more than a river can break out of its banks unless more water pours into it from a more powerful source.

We wear down unless we are tuned to the song of the universe.

Gretchen is a friend who has a rich sense of imagery. She once shared a dream with me which seemed to her a metaphor of her soul's journey as it has become more attuned. She dreamed that she was with a great many dogs, each one barking with excitement as it ran everywhere, chasing squirrels and cats and sniffing up old bones, each one following its own trail, casting furiously and frantically about. This exhausted them; they fell in a heap. Then they scented something! Heading off in the same direction together, they followed a wonderful smell which led them to a lake of pure water from which they drank deeply. Refreshed, they set off as a unit to climb a great hill. Gretchen remembers vividly what it felt like: she and her dogs were a team, their energy harnessed for something sublime.

Attunement occurs when we focus ourselves so that our energy begins to open to the single direction of God. So long as we are like Gretchen's dogs, casting restlessly in many places, it is hard for us to become attuned. Our energy is aimlessly disposed, at the beck and call of the world or of our own changing moods. Something must draw us which is compelling enough to pull together our scattered lives, to open us to the process of growth about which we spoke in the last chapter.

What we need is powerful energy to move us beyond the magnetic vortexes we create and from which we can't escape all by ourselves. We need to tune ourselves to a ray of grace and light that is greater than our own power. Paradoxically, we find that while the power source, God, is far more than anything we can drum up, it also lives in our depths. The more we are attuned to God, the more we become ourselves. God and we, by a very great mystery, cannot be separated from each other. The more God lives in us, the more we become distinct, separate, unique and special persons. Such is the nature of divine love which takes such delight in empowering its creatures.

I remember sitting in meditation with a group of others when this struck home in that gentle and compelling way which I have come to believe is one of the signs of God's presence. I came to the group that day with no particular feeling of inner inspiration—only a prayer that I might tune in to God as much as possible. As we meditated, I began to get a sense of a subtle, loving presence slowly opening up my inner life. There was nothing alien or strange about this presence; rather it was as though I was being reintroduced to deeper levels of life which I had always known were there but which I had forgotten. In the most gentle of ways, my heart felt as though it was expanding. It was as though I was being attuned to the life of a Greater One than I, into a broader consciousness and loving perspective, and yet, as this happened, I found myself more and more clearly me, even more an individual and more empowered. I didn't disappear, my problems didn't go away, but I got a different outlook on them. I felt that I was in Christ and Christ was in me. This was nothing I could manufacture by my own efforts. I could only be intensely receptive to it. I was being attuned and realigned to a power far beyond me and yet which, by the grace of God, was working within me as well.

Attunement to God is like fine-tuning a radio to a classical music station on FM. There are all kinds of messages coming through the airways—some pretty good, some utterly dismal. To get a station that plays Bach can take some effort. The station you are searching for may always be broadcasting, but it may be hard to pick up without just the right sort of tuning. The spiritual life is like that. There are all sorts of "broadcasts" in life, some glorious and some that are destructive to the human spirit. To align with the Spirit takes some fine tuning, particularly if we have been listening for years without discrimination.

Swami Kriyananda compares life without this sort of spiritual attunement to being in the middle of a large, dark building at night. The floor is littered with hundreds of obstacles and is broken in many places. Without some kind of light, it would be impossible to reach safety. Or, he says, it is like being a prisoner in a labyrinth—its hopelessly complex maze leading to dead end after dead end. In the Greek myth of Theseus, Ariadne gave Theseus a thread to unwind before he entered the labyrinth to fight the Minotaur. Without the thread of attunement to the Spirit, we come to a dead end. With it, we find our souls' desire. As Kriyananda says:

> Imagine mighty rivers of consciousness flowing through the universe—sweeping through vast stellar systems, engulfing planets, catching up in swirling currents the little thoughts, ideas, and passions of men. . . . Men imagine that it is they who create history. As well might the little

leaf, bobbing lightly on the water's surface, think to determine the river's course! Free will does indeed exist, but not as most people imagine it—not, that is to say, in private, egoic isolation from the universe. Freedom must be sought, rather, in broader realities. Man is free only in the sense that he can choose his influences. Each one can determine which, out of an infinity of streams of universal consciousness, he will enter.

The rivers of history are extraordinarily powerful. The great majority of men and women, failing to tune in to them consciously, are swept helplessly, hither and yon, by the merest ripples. Geniuses, on the other hand, may—and saints invariably do—flow serenely and joyously with the flood until they reach the ocean of cosmic consciousness and freedom. . . . Ordinary man, caught up in fads of the moment, drifts passively more often than not into stagnant by-waters, from which death alone rescues him at last. Instead of the freedom claimed by him as his inalienable human "right," he achieves mere bondage to outwardness, and to ego.

Those, however, who attune themselves to these great streams of consciousness achieve greatness themselves. This is true of genius. It is even truer of spiritual greatness. As the Bible puts it, "As many as received him, to them gave he the power to become the sons of God."[1]

If we could only realize it, the Divine One whom we seek is within us and all around us. When we are out of tune, imprisoned by our problems, it often seems that we are separate from God or that God is too preoccupied or too remote to pay much attention to us except in rare moments. It's as though we imagine that God is a heavenly telephone receptionist who is very busy attending to many things and many people. Attunement, therefore, would seem to require that we get God's attention by luck and effort. If we are lucky, and very, very good, God may listen to us—but maybe not more than once or twice a month because God is too busy to plug us in more frequently.

The truth, I believe, is very different.

When we see Christ, we know that God hasn't left us alone to manage all by ourselves. God isn't far away, preoccupied with running a great cosmic switchboard. We are loved, forgiven, reclaimed and energized. Christ brings God's light to earth to restore and guide souls who are lost in spiritual darkness. At-one-ment occurs.

What we experience as we become attuned to Christ is that with all the creatures of this universe, we live and move and have our very being in God's own life. We are being brought forth each moment as God fills creation with himself. All things are from God and in God. Attunement doesn't involve competing for God's attention; it means opening ourselves up to that union which we already have with the Divine One and cooperating with God as valued partners in the process of becoming filled up and rounded out. Attunement means making room in ourselves for the Divine Life which wants more and more to radiate outward to express itself. It's like breathing air into a tight, small bag so that it becomes a wonderful, richly colored balloon. Molecules that have been constricted now have space and freedom. The balloon becomes what it was designed to be—only unlike a balloon we get to join in the fun.

One of the most powerful stories I have heard was that of a woman who had a near-death experience. At first, looking at her body from above while a health team of physicians and nurses was trying to resuscitate her, she then became aware of a great, brilliant presence, "a light stronger than a thousand suns" which held her in such love that she felt more whole than she had ever been. In that loving presence, which she believed was God, she reviewed every event of her life and then was given a choice to come back or move on. She chose to come back. Ever since, she has been living with a different focus. She learned that what is more important than anything else in life is staying attuned to that presence: "Because it is homeland of all of us and when you have experienced what I did, you live with so much more joy, and you care so much more about the basic things: God, loving people and the simple pleasures."

That's what attunement does. It opens us to the Divine One. Our focus shifts. We are aware that under life as we normally perceive it, there is a deeper stratum, the light and love of God. Even if we forget it or imagine it does not exist, it is there. As we begin to become more attuned to it, we get hints of what it feels like to be truly at home in this universe. We are less fragmented. Faith becomes more than blind hope; it becomes an actual experience of the presence of the Holy One. Life continues to challenge us just as much but we move into those challenges with less resentment. Our hearts open another notch; we don't have to be told to love as much as we cooperate in the process of letting a larger power of love do its work in us. Our sins become more obvious and our shame is heightened for so many things we have messed up, but strangely those sins become lighter as well, unable to possess us with the same power as before.

How do we become attuned? We definitely have a vital role to play; we don't wait passively for God to do all the work. As a matter of fact, God looks for signals from us which show that we want to be attuned. It doesn't require arid and arduous methods, but it does take sincerity, intention and willingness. This is what spiritual practices are all about— they are not intended to be grim tasks which oppress our spirits but our way of cooperating with the divine plan of filling people with the life of God. This can happen in many ways—from prayer and meditation, to study of the scriptures, to songs which open up our hearts. We use them to make room for God.

We use these things to clean our windows. For years the window that is us has been covered with grime too thick to let God's light come clearly through. So we try to keep the commandments, we make ways for the Spirit to find inroads in us, we pray, we serve, we live in a spiritual family which keeps us company on a common journey and, with that family, open ourselves to the power of sacrament and word. As difficult as it is, we simplify our lives as much as possible so there is time and room to be with God. We go for help when we need it from others. Without such things it is not possible to stay open to the emanations of divine life.

Behind all those ways of re-presenting ourselves to God, one theme stands forth when we look at the lives of great saints: attunement means practicing the presence of God in the midst of daily life.

Brother Lawrence, a seventeenth century Frenchman, spent twenty-five years in a Carmelite community where he served in various menial roles, mostly in the kitchen, but he became known throughout Europe for his wonderful experience of God's immediate presence. He was in touch with God. He knew God. He lived in the presence of God every day. People from every background, eager to find a similar vitality and certainty in their own lives, wrote him letters. To all he gave the same answer: attune yourself to God. What he meant by this is learn how to live as though God is beside you and with you all the time—as in fact God is.

> . . . spend the remainder of your life only in worshipping God. He lays no great burden upon us: a little remembrance of Him from time to time; a little adoration; sometimes to pray for His grace, sometimes to offer Him your sorrows and sometimes to return to Him thanks for the benefits He has given you, and still gives you, in the midst of your troubles. He asks you to console yourself with Him the oftenest you can. Lift up your heart to Him at your meals and when you are in company; the least little remembrance will always be acceptable to Him. You need not cry very loud; He is nearer to us than we think.

> To be with God, there is no need to be continually in church. We may make an oratory of our heart wherein to retire from time to time to converse with Him in meekness, humility, and love. Everyone is capable of such

familiar conversation with God, some more, some less. He knows what we can do. Let us begin, then. Perhaps He is just waiting for one generous resolution on our part.[2]

Out of nineteenth century Russia has come a remarkable book about the journeys of a person who calls himself a "pilgrim." Traveling from place to place in Russia and Siberia, he shares his travel notes with simple charm and directness. But there is a deeper journey. He learns and practices the Jesus Prayer, saying with the rise and fall of his breath, "Lord Jesus Christ, have mercy on me." An ancient prayer, going back centuries in the Orthodox Church, it is taken up by the pilgrim as a way to pray without ceasing in his heart as well as his mind during his travels. It becomes for him, as it has been for many, a way of attuning himself constantly to God. Far more than a technique, it is deeply devotional and intentional, representing the constant yearning of the heart for God. As the Bishop of Truro says in an introduction to *The Way of the Pilgrim*:

[The pilgrim] harps very much on one string . . . but what a string it is!—a deep bourdon-sound, which runs on, underneath the harmonies and discords of daily life, till it has brought them into unison with God.[3]

Paramahansa Yogananda, the author of *Autobiography of a Yogi*, was one of the greatest souls India has sent to the west. A spiritual master, he inspired many to attune themselves so completely to God that they became saints themselves. Sri Daya Mata, one of his leading disciples, speaks about his impact:

Yesterday some of us were reminiscing about Master and the great inspiration he was to all of us. That aura of dignity could never have been around him if he had merely imagined it. Reading books or hearing lectures does not give one spirituality. Only by living the spiritual life does one become as Master was.

[He] used to say, When you are working, make your work a form of meditation. Don't waste your time in idle thoughts or talk. Every now and then think, 'Lord, it is Your power that operates these hands. Your power throbs in this heart. Your power allows me to think.' The more you meditate upon these thoughts, the more you live within your Self, in that world which lies within, the more you become in tune with that Divine One who is throbbing in every cell of every living thing.[4]

Attunement is not a matter of concentrating on our own perfectibility as much as upon God's perfection. We look to God. We try to open to God. We direct our inner yearning toward God whenever we can, no matter what we are doing. We go to God with our joys, our hurts, our problems. Recollection of the Presence like this is a critical turning point in our inner lives. Nearly anyone can remember God and converse with the Lord now and again. When we are able to do it more often, and then still more often, a great event is taking place in our souls. When we operate from the egotistical part of ourselves, the inner conversation within ourselves—what we are feeling and thinking and experiencing—is inspired by little else than self-concern. When our attunement becomes more God-directed, there is a transformation of our inner dialogue. We gradually learn to share with God whatever we are feeling. Slowly, as we learn to trust ourselves to the Beloved One, our horizons broaden. Our perspective deepens. We begin to experience God communion more frequently. On one level we may be carrying on the demands of daily life but behind the scenes, at a profounder level, we are learning to make room for the great ocean of God's life to expand our souls.

Do we forget to attune to God? Of course. Persistence is called for and so is patience and humor. But it is a natural process and God is our ally. We find that while once we had to swim hard, as time goes on we are increasingly upheld by divine currents. Communion with God is natural to us. All of us have the capacity to experience sustained awareness of the Divine Presence.

The witness of people such as Brother Lawrence, the Russian pilgrim, Yogananda and a host of others is that attunement leads to wholeness. We don't all begin at the same place but we all can find, as they did, that the more we open ourselves, the more God draws us. Increasingly, a single-pointed resolve stirs within us. We find that we want to become more steady on our paths, lifting more of who we are and what the world is into the Divine Light. As we do so, we awaken to our true nature.

What opens us up isn't so much what we are now but what we are willing to attune ourselves to.

MEDITATION, THE WAY OF INNER COMMUNION

Archbishop Anthony Bloom tells a story about a seeker. Shortly after Father Bloom's ordination an elderly person came to see him about her prayer life. He recommended that she talk to those more experienced than he, but she responded that in spite of their reputed knowledge about the spiritual life, such persons had never given her a sensible reply, so she had decided to ask him, since by chance he might blunder out the right thing! So he offered what he could. He said that if she spoke all the time she wouldn't give God a chance to place a word in. He recommended that she go to her room, put it in order, sit in her armchair, look around and take stock of where she lived, and then simply knit for fifteen minutes before the face of God, trying to enjoy the peace of the room.

She didn't think this was very pious advice but she tried it. After a while she came to see him. "It works," she said. "What works?" Bloom asked because he was curious too! She replied that she did just what he advised, settling in her armchair after breakfast and loving the notion that she had fifteen minutes to do nothing without being guilty. She looked around and found what a nice room she lived in and then began to feel quiet because it was so peaceful. Then she knit before the face of God. She is telling Father Anthony about her experience:

> And I became more and more aware of the silence. The needles hit the armrest of my chair, the clock was ticking peacefully, there was nothing to bother about, I had no need of straining myself, and then I perceived that this silence was not simply an absence of noise, but that the silence had substance. It was not absence of something but presence of something. The silence had a density, a richness, and it began to pervade me. The silence around

began to come and meet the silence in me." And then in the end she said something very beautiful which I have found later in the French writer, Georges Bernanos. She said, "All of a sudden I perceived that the silence was a presence. At the heart of the silence there was He who is all stillness, all peace, all poise."[1]

There is at the heart of silence a Sacred Presence. Somewhere, sometime, we have heard its echo in our hearts. We'd like more of it, but we tell ourselves that someday, when we have fewer responsibilities, we'll find ways to tune in more often. Or, we tell ourselves, only great saints or people off in desert retreats have the luxury of cultivating it. The rest of us, we say with a sigh, can only experience it on rare occasions.

It's not true. The world is full of people who seek attunement to God through meditation and who mine rich treasures.

The great religions of the world have all said that meditation is a powerful and essential way to open ourselves to God. They know that even a little of it can create personal and subtle changes in a person's life. This is true for Christians, too. From the time Jesus withdrew for a time from crowds to commune with his heavenly Father until now, thousands upon thousands of his followers have sat before the face of God where they have experienced the touch of God's presence and the infinite bliss of God's love and have been healed.

Christians know this and want more of it. Why else did Jesus give us the eucharist? He came to dwell in us so that we could dwell in him—in profound inner communion. Indeed, the purpose of the eucharist has much in common with the purpose of meditation—to lead us into nothing less than intimate communion with the Lord. Unfortunately, people forget that holy communion is literally holy communion. It's my conviction that as people learn to meditate, they will be able to claim at even more profound levels that which awaits them in the holy feast.

Thomas Keating has pointed out that for the first fifteen

centuries of the Church's life, a positive attitude characterized the church's teaching about meditation.* With scripture reading and prayer, meditation—the experience of opening oneself to inner communion with God—often took place during the same period of prayer. Only during the past few centuries have Christians thought that it was reserved for a few advanced souls, most of whom lived in monasteries. It was admired from a distance, but many were taught that it wasn't something to which the ordinary Christian, clergy or layperson, should aspire.

The genuine Christian tradition, taught without hesitation during the first fifteen centuries, is that meditation is a normal and essential part of the spiritual life and open to everyone.[2] I believe it is time for us to reclaim that heritage.

In recent years there has been great interest in recovering that legacy. Partially this has come about through the influence of eastern religions; by learning of the great mystics and saints of other traditions, Christians have begun to come back to their own tradition. They are reclaiming their legacy which recognizes that direct inner communion with God is possible and which says that religion includes but is ever so much more than good doctrine or good works. We are seeing a great move to recover the church's contemplative heritage. Churches and seminaries are teaching courses in spirituality. Religious bookstores are full of classical and contemporary publications about the spiritual life. Centers such as Shalem in Washington, D.C. are springing up to teach contemplative spirituality as well as to train persons as spiritual directors. Retreat houses across the country are full every weekend. Prayerful exercises of interiority such as "centering prayer" are being taught through

---

*In this book, I use the term meditation to mean the same thing as the ancient Christian word "contemplation." Until recently in the Christian tradition, "meditation" has often referred to intellectual and emotional engagement with scripture, as in the Ignatian disciplines, rather than meditation as it has come to be popularly understood, namely, as contemplative attention to the presence of God.

books and conferences. However they are going about their search, people are expressing their desire to go beyond a shallow sense of prayer as a hotline in times of difficulty to a way of experiencing God as a living reality in their own lives. Learning how to meditate is at the heart of this movement because, as Keating says, "[Meditation] is a resting in God. In this resting or stillness the mind and heart are . . . beginning to experience, to taste, what they have been seeking. This places them in a state of tranquillity and profound interior peace. This state is not the suspension of all action, but a mingling of a few simple acts to sustain one's attention to God with the loving experience of God's presence."[3]

First, let's clear the decks about what meditation is not. Is meditation an escape from "real life"? For a few, perhaps so, but true meditation is not escape; it means consenting to enter a relationship with no less than God. Meditation isn't a form of self-hypnosis either. We don't make God present when we meditate or pray. We open ourselves to the One who is already among us. Nor is meditation a form of mental blankness; it's a receptive state of inner awareness where we make room for God to roll up his sleeves and go to work in us. Finally, meditation is not, as some unfortunately believe, a method that makes space for Satan. Just the reverse: it softens up the junk of our false selves—our compulsions and fixations—so we can make space for the healing power of the Holy Spirit.

What is it that meditation can help us open to? This is a good place to remind ourselves of that to which the great mystics point. Here is Blessed Henry Suso:

> In the first days of his conversion it happened upon the Feast of St. Agnes . . . that the Servitor went into the choir. He was alone . . . and he was in much suffering, for a heavy trouble weighed upon his heart. . . . Then did he see and hear that which no tongue can express.
>
> That which the Servitor saw had no form neither any manner of being; yet he had of it a joy such as he might

have known in the seeing of the shapes and substances of all joyful things. His heart was hungry, yet satisfied, his soul was full of contentment and joy; his prayers and hopes were all fulfilled. And the Friar could do naught but contemplate this Shining Brightness. . . . Then he said, "If that which I see and feel be not the Kingdom of Heaven, I know not what it can be: for it is very sure that the endurance of all possible pains were but a poor price to pay for the eternal possession of so great a joy.[4]

Here is Blaise Pascal, the great French mathematician. What follows was written on a scrap of parchment, sewn up in his doublet, and found by a servant at his death: a perpetual remembrance of his initiation into Reality:

From about half-past ten in the evening until about half-past twelve

FIRE

God of Abraham, God of Isaac, God of Jacob, not of the philosophers and savants.

Certitude. Certitude. Feeling. Joy. Peace. God of Jesus Christ. My God and thy God. Thy God shall be my God. . . .[5]

This is Fritjof Capra, a modern scientist:

Five years ago, I had a beautiful experience which set me on a road that has led to the writing of this book. I was sitting by the ocean one late summer afternoon, watching the waves rolling in and feeling the rhythm of my breathing, when I suddenly became aware of my whole environment as being engaged in a gigantic cosmic dance. Being a physicist, I knew that the sand, rocks, water and air around me were made of vibrating molecules and atoms, and that these consisted of particles. I knew also that the Earth's atmosphere was continually bombarded by showers of "cosmic rays." . . . All this was familiar to me from my research in high-energy physics, but until that moment I had only experienced it through graphs, diagrams and mathematical theories. As I sat on that beach my former experiences came to life; I "saw" cascades of energy coming down from outer space, in which particles were created and destroyed in rhythmic pulses; I "saw" the atoms of the elements and those of my body participating in this cosmic dance of energy: I felt the rhythm and I "heard" its sound. . . .[6]

The universe is on fire with God, and those who meditate sometimes may experience that fire, but it is important to be clear that meditation does not necessarily lead into experiences of Reality like this. Indeed, meditators learn to let go of the need for "supernatural" experiences. Drawing closer to God can or cannot issue in such phenomena. Meditation is not a technique to "get" such experiences because it is not phenomena as such that we are after but God, and God comes to us as a free agent, on God's own terms with God's own wisdom about what is congruent for each soul. I quote the mystics because they remind us that we are grounded in an incredible Reality every moment of our lives which we so often miss in our self-preoccupation. We are part of a divine, cosmic dance! We live in the grace of God and the love of God! That is the truth of things, and it is our destiny to enter into communion with this Reality.

What does meditation do? It invites the energy of the Spirit to flow more powerfully into us. Someone has suggested that we think of God and ourselves like the light bulb and slides in a slide projector. God is the light bulb. The habit patterns of our lives are like slides. If the slides are full of reactive and harmful stuff, the images cast on the screen of our lives are distortions of the light. The energy of the Spirit moves through us because there is ultimately only one energy in the universe which is Spirit, but what comes out of us depends on the quality of the patterns we hold before the screen. Our goal in meditation is to cultivate a more transparent, unblemished way of offering ourselves into the light. When we meditate and direct our attention to God, we allow the light from the Spirit to move more directly through us with more power and less deflection.

There are many ways to meditate. The kind I speak about in this book uses a word or image as a way to open to God's presence and is largely based on Centering Prayer which has been introduced so successfully in our time by Thomas Keating and Basil Pennington and which is based on *The Cloud of Unknowing* by an anonymous fourteenth century Christian spiritual master. It, like most forms of meditation, operates on two basic assumptions. The first is that God is, and the universe trembles with Sacred Presence. This means that we don't have to bring God close because God is already close, hidden just behind that which passes for reality to our waking consciousness. The second assumption says that because we are the very sons and daughters of God we have every right to address God as a great master frequently did when he said, "Reveal thyself. You are here; you can't fool me. I want more of you in my life!" We do this by removing the obstacles which keep us from allowing God's grace to operate more freely in us and which prevent us from living out of our true state of abiding union with the Beloved One.

Centering Prayer is based on a gentle but constant focus on the presence of God by the use of a word, a short phrase or an image. The technique is simple though not always easy. It involves centering our attention and concern on God. With deep faith we move into awareness of the Presence who is here among us. A word or short phrase is chosen such as "God" or "Heavenly Father" or "Divine Mother" or "Jesus" or "Love" or "Beloved" or "Abba" or "Peace" or "Amen" or "My God, My All" to bring the restless mind to focus and, more importantly, to serve as the focal point for one's concern and love. Or, for some who are especially drawn to visualization, mental images may be used such as light or an inner picture of Jesus.

I find, before I begin meditation, that it is always important to start with prayer. As well as I can, I offer the moments to come to God no matter what kind of meditation may follow—whether filled with a sense of the Sacred Presence or dry as a bone. And then, at least during the opening moments of meditation as I move from the busyness of my day into a quieter time, I often find it helpful to become more still and intentional by working with my breath. Often, I begin by inhaling very slowly and deeply, imagining that I am not only inhaling air but the peace, joy and power of God. I visualize that breath filling not only my lungs but my whole body, starting at my feet and culminating in my head, especially at the point between the eyebrows. As I exhale, I release my life into the care of God. This exercise can be repeated six to twelve times. Then when I am ready I move into a time of centering prayer, using my sacred word or phrase. Finally, at the close of the meditation, I usually pray for others, for the world and for myself, becoming a channel for God's healing energy to move beyond me into God's larger creation. My final prayer is the Lord's Prayer.

The purpose of meditation is to offer oneself into God's presence. It is as though God is just on the other side of a little door. The door only opens from God's side; God is free to do what is best for us. God opens the door when it is right for us and in ways that are appropriate on any given occasion. The reason we meditate is to knock, to show God we mean business and to place ourselves as receptively as we can before the Holy One so that the Spirit will find a ready welcome. What we find is that the Lord has been knocking all along, hoping to gain entrance. "Behold, I stand at the door and knock."

Meditation like this is different than intellectualizing or figuring out whether God exists. It is the difference, for example, between talking with someone about the nature and person of Christ and coming into his presence. We can't zap God into existence by meditating or even by meditating harder. I often ask people in my classes to imagine that they are carrying on a great theological debate about whether the resurrection is true when Christ walks through the door, cutting through all our words about him and joining us in person. As

Thomas did we might exclaim, "My Lord and my God!" When we meditate, we join Thomas; we use a phrase to help us recollect that God is with us (even if we may not experience it at the time). It is not the word or image as such that is important or even the technique; what matters is the Divine Reality to whom we are orienting ourselves.

In spite of what people sometimes think, meditation isn't mysterious or exotic. Its purpose is the same as the purpose of everything in the spiritual life: becoming open to the Presence. To paraphrase Thomas Keating, meditation is a way of telling God, "Here you are and here I am; I want you but how this happens is up to you." We frequently wander and go to other things in our minds, but gently we call ourselves back to focus and once again rest in the One who, mysteriously, is praying in us even as we contemplate the Beloved. Generally, throughout our meditation, we will stay with our sacred word or image as we gather ourselves in the Presence, perhaps we may momentarily cry, "Lord, I want thee" or "Lord, I love thee," or perhaps, if our minds wander, we may address God honestly to tell God that our attention is on other things, but then we come back to a focused state of receptivity, gathering our desire into the word or image that seems best able to sum up God's presence to us and our intention to be with the Gracious One. Perhaps a sense of divine presence steals over us, perhaps there is a heightened attunement to God's will, perhaps there are none of the above. Perhaps we will move into silence, for even the sacred word itself has become intrusive so that we find ourselves becoming one with the very essence of that to which our attention is directed. Then, even as Christ, we discover that we are coming forth from God and returning to God. Nothing but God holds sway.

In the last chapter I talked about the centrality of attunement for the spiritual journey. Meditation is a focused time of attunement. It is not a mere technique or the repetition of a sacred word. God is sending us great blessings but we must do our part by holding a receptive, welcoming attitude. We must receive the Lord's life in our souls, in no way straining but trustingly attuning ourselves to God's life. As Jesus said, "He who abides in me, and I in him, he it is that bears much fruit . . ." (Jn 15:5 RSV). We are tuning forks. We are sensitizing our consciousness to God's consciousness, our hearts to God's heart, our wills to God's will. We are deepening our awareness of God so that it permeates every part of our being. Perhaps, at the end of our meditation, if our consciousness has been enlarged, we may seek guidance from a fuller perspective. Finally, we try to carry the attunement raised in meditation into the rest of the day.

Sometimes people believe that meditation is supposed to lead to the suppression of all thought. Certainly our minds can become quieter, but it is doubtful that on most occasions all our thoughts will be left behind. Notice them as they go by; just don't get hooked by them. Nor is the purpose to move into blankness (though you may become very quiet inside); the intention is to be in God's presence.

What about distractions? Everyone experiences them. Our minds, liking to stay in control, play all kinds of tricks to divert us until they know we mean business—and even then they come back to test us! Sometimes the mind even wants us to become angry at it by scolding it for running off onto other things; that way it won't have to return to the business at hand. Treat it with perfect but firm courtesy. The mind and emotions are an important part of who we are; our thoughts and feelings are given their due but they learn that it is not them to which we are giving our primary attention. Even as we notice what passes through us, we move back to the depths.

There is a profound lesson here for life. Meditation is less a technique than it is a metaphor for spiritual living throughout the day. We are pulled by a thousand compulsions and distractions. That which is stuck in us doesn't want to give way to higher things. To make room for God is to let go of lesser securities, to soften up the hard crust of that which is false in us. Learning to let everything go by in meditation but our attention to God is a way to learn to let go of anything in daily life which is less than God.

Still, there are times when one needs to use the distractions as sacred words themselves. If, for example, there is something that keeps coming to the front of your mind which refuses to pass on, it can be helpful to share it with God. God is not the stranger to reality that we are. It may help to experience feelings of pain or fear as they come and offer them as your prayer word. Sometimes people believe that the use of meditation means that they are supposed to avoid their problems by repressing their feelings. This is not called for. As the psychotherapists know, keeping problems and feelings buried in the subconscious will not eradicate them. They exist and their energy is powerful. Usually it is enough simply to see and notice what the mind brings up and returns to God through the sacred image, but sometimes we need to share problems and feelings more directly. This can deepen the relationship with God and free us up. Whatever is experienced can be directed to God as One who can understand, share, care and guide us toward appropriate action. This intentional offering of what is present is in itself a sacred word when it takes us into God's presence.

As time goes along the meditator becomes aware that many of his issues regarding distraction or other struggles with meditation come from parts of his life that are at last ready to surface. Sometimes disturbing thoughts come. Sometimes old memories well up. This is natural; indeed it is usually a sign that blocked energy is being freed up. God is healing us. That which has been stuck in us, including unresolved issues of security, esteem or power that go back for years, begins to loosen up.

Meditation opens many doors into the personality. Many persons in our culture, for example, have considerable anxiety about performance and feel that if they are not meditating well, either God is not truly present after all or they can't keep up with others for whom meditation is easier. Frustration emerges. Feelings of anger contend with feelings of self-doubt. The temptation to quit is strong.

Such times are great opportunities for spiritual and psychological development because God is helping us see what is illusory in our lives. If a person is hooked by perfection and performance, this is a real opportunity to notice the problem, place it before God and ask for help in understanding its roots. Then, usually at a time other than meditation, one can search out the origins of the problem.

A friend who has struggled with performance issues in many aspects of his life brought those struggles into his time of meditation too. An achiever, he believed that if he only meditated well enough, using good technique and conscientiously following the meditative instructions he had received in just the right way, he would be successful. He found that he could not engineer the process. After hitting a brick wall, he nearly gave up in disgust. At the crossroads, he could walk away in frustration or let go in trust that God was there in any case and was helping him with the very issue that was most difficult for him. He decided to stick it out. As time passed, he realized that God was much more willing to let him grow by degrees than his perfectionistic parents had been able to. After a while, a helpful image came to him: he imagined that he was near the outlet of a great reservoir of water. "When meditation comes easily to me," he later said, "it's not hard for me to believe I am able to bathe in the water coming from that reservoir, but when it doesn't go well, I think the reservoir has dried up. That's changing. I am beginning to sense that no matter what my prayer-time is like, the water is always there. I'm learning to trust that and center myself in God as though that's true even when I don't feel it's true." His issue in meditation was his issue in life. As he learned to trust God throughout the ups and downs of his contemplative time, he was also being healed of an old problem in his life pattern.

More than anything else in meditation, we are trying to be open to where we already are—in God's presence. We can't make spiritual things happen. We can use meditation to place ourselves before God, making space for the Gracious One to heal us as God knows best. Our willingness to be in communion with God can assume different textures. Most of the time it involves letting go of everything but attention to God through the use of the sacred word or visualization, trustingly making room for God's presence. Occasionally it comes with all the passion the heart can muster, crying for God to heal us and to fill us. Sometimes it involves offering God what we are feeling and thinking. In all cases meditation involves the focus of our attention on God and our desire to love God and be open to God's presence no matter what. With that comes powerful healing.

In what passes for "ordinary" consciousness, our awareness of the Divine Presence is obscured. We live in a divided state of separation and even enmity. Meditation can lead us back to the truth of our abiding union with God. Because of what it helps us experience, we find that in addition to a growing sense of God's presence, important things are coming to life in us which are the fruits of that presence: more compassion, an increasing freedom from our compulsions, and, above all, more love for God and God's ways.

We begin to understand first-hand what it means to be in communion with God. And we wonder why we waited so long.

Here is a guided meditation from Thomas Keating:

> We begin our prayer by disposing our body. Let it be relaxed and calm, but inwardly alert. . . .
>
> We are . . . present now, with the whole of our being, in complete openness . . . The past and future—time itself—are forgotten. We are here in the presence of the Ultimate Mystery. Like the air we breathe, this divine Presence is all around us and within us, distinct from us, but never separate from us. . . .
>
> Without effort . . . we sink into this Presence, letting everything else go. Let love alone speak: the simple desire

to be one with the Presence, to forget self, and to rest in the Ultimate Mystery.

This Presence is so immense, yet so humble; awe-inspiring, yet so gentle; limitless, yet so intimate, tender and personal. I know that I am known. Everything in my life is transparent in this Presence. It knows everything about me—all my weaknesses, brokenness, sinfulness— and still loves me infinitely. This Presence is healing, strengthening, refreshing—just by its Presence. It is non-judgmental, self-giving, seeking no reward, boundless in compassion. It is like coming home to a place I should never have left, to an awareness that was somehow always there, but which I did not recognize. I cannot force this awareness or bring it about. A door opens within me, but from the other side. . . .

We wait patiently; in silence, openness, and quiet expectancy. . . . We surrender to the attraction to be still, to be loved, just to be. . . .[7]

SERVICE

Peter was sitting in the waiting room of a city hospital while his wife was in exploratory surgery. The fences that people build between themselves were gone. Whenever a doctor appeared to tell a relative in the waiting room how surgery had gone, everyone became quiet and listened. If the news was good, there was applause and congratulations. If the news was grim, there was empathy. Coffee was passed around and people nearest the one who had received such a message reached a hand over to touch her or him. Instant community was built around common need.

The depth of community that was reached so quickly at that hospital is unusual. We are living in a time when people feel cut off from one another. There is no special or urgent purpose in the air. Some recall the 1960s with nostalgia because groups of people were gathered around common causes such as the fight for civil rights. Now, most of us follow our own paths, look after our own interests, and join with others, if we join at all, on a smaller scale. Add to this a deep sense of foreboding about nuclear war, environmental contamination, drugs, the gap between the "haves" and the "have nots," and terrorism, and the result is a feeling of powerlessness—even during those times when we may be fairly successful in dealing with the issues of our immediate, day to day lives. Peter's experience in the waiting room was special because it took him to a level not always experienced these days.

The challenge of the call to service in the late twentieth century is a challenge to find empowerment for service. Only something compelling enough to enlist the deepest part of the human spirit and to lift us beyond our marrow-deep angst can move us from our narrow self-interest. Peter saw something of this when common sympathy bound strangers together in a waiting room. That was a metaphor of the human need for connection at important levels of meaning and mutual care. It gives a hint of what we need most of all. We have a desperate need for abiding resources deep enough to help us find sustained compassion and connection.

The basic issue is spiritual. Only when we are rooted in something transcendent can we find sustained resources to keep our hearts open. For that is what we need. If the heart is not sustained by spiritual power and spiritual discipline, we fall prey to the lesser spirits of greed, undue self-importance, violence, dependence on the opinion of others, overweening attachment to things less than Spirit to give us meaning, and defensiveness. Under all these destructive spirits is fear. We fear we are nothing and so must create vast amounts of clutter about ourselves to be something. And of course it doesn't work.

It's not just those who have no spiritual grounding who need spiritual power and discipline to keep their hearts open. Without spiritual discipline, even those who are spiritually oriented fall into difficulty and even despair because they burn out. By ourselves we are simply unable to carry the banner of compassion indefinitely. There was a time not long ago in mainline Christian churches where the persons most passionate about social action regarded prayer as escapist. That is changing. There is a growing understanding of the need to reach deeper than good intentions. We are seeing that long-term power comes from staying connected to a deeper reality than our own energies.

Henri Nouwen has said:

> One danger I see among nuclear and social protesters, although I support their work totally, is that they can become so dominated by their fear of tomorrow that they miss the gift of the hour. The reality of today does not become a source of liberation for them. They then can become tainted by the very demon they are fighting, and soon they can find themselves turning hateful, aggressive, and violent. You can fight against death only in the strength of life, in God's presence now. [1]

Our greatest hope that service to the world won't be neglected comes when we encounter people who stay open to the presence of God. An outstanding example is Thomas Merton who, just because he was a monk, could personify for some their worst fears that spirituality equates with withdrawal from the world. Merton was a contemplative monk and he was also a social activist, a poet, a bridge between western and eastern religious thought, and a passionate human being. Whatever he wrote or did as an activist was forged on the anvil of his interior life with God. He would be the first to say there is nothing that can touch one's first-hand experience of the vivid reality of God's love for the world for keeping one from shutting down and closing off. When we are grounded in God, we know there is far more to live for than the stock market and football scores. When we are out of touch with God, it can be even easier for self-importance to become too important, for fences to be built between us and others, and for selfishness to rule our spirits.

There is no substitute in this world for knowing that we live with a generous God who never will stop loving us and caring for us. When we really take that in, something opens in us. Henri Nouwen is on target again when he says:

> If we are to be peacemakers, it is essential that we take on what I would like to call a mentality of abundance and put away from us the mentality of scarcity. This sense of scarcity makes us desperate, and we turn to competition, hoarding, and a kind of parody of self-preservation. This greed extends not only to material goods but also to knowledge, friendships, and ideas. We worry that everything we possess is threatened. This is especially true in a society that grows more affluent, experiences more opportunities for hoarding and more fears of losing what has been stored, and in the process creates enemies and wars.[2]

"Our God gives in good measure, pressed down, shaken together and running over" (Lk 6:36–38). It is when we actually experience this for ourselves that we better learn to let go of our need to build so many fences and guard our lives so carefully. When we know God first-hand, other things lose their death grip on us. We don't need so much to keep us safe. I believe a great legacy of the saints is their knowledge that fear loses much of its power when we stay in touch with our spiritual homeland. The saints are human, they experience what it means to be afraid, they move back and forth between what it is to be involved in the abundant life of God and what is it to live outside of God's domain, but above everything they are empowered by the Divine Source. From that profound center has come their power to impact the world.

I am deeply moved by the story of Martin Luther King, Jr. Shortly after Dr. King was arrested for the first time during the Montgomery bus boycott, he returned home and experienced a wave of fear and pressure. Late in the night he received a hate phone call. He couldn't sleep and paced the floor, terribly aware of incredible pressures—the hatred of white people and the crushing needs and hopes of so many black people who looked to him for leadership.

> King buried his face in his hands at the kitchen table. He admitted to himself that he was afraid, that he had nothing left, that the people would falter if they looked to him for strength. Then he said as much out loud. He spoke the name of no deity, but his doubts spilled out as a prayer, ending, "I've come to the point where I can't face it alone." As he spoke these words, the fears suddenly began to melt away. He became intensely aware of what he called an "inner voice" telling him to do what he thought was right. Such simplicity worked miracles, bringing a shudder of relief and the courage to face anything. It was for King the first transcendent religious experience of his life. . . . For King, the moment awakened and confirmed his belief that the essence of religion was not a grand metaphysical idea but something personal, grounded in experience—something that opened up mysteriously beyond the predicaments of human beings in their frailest and noblest moments.[3]

When Mother Teresa says, "I see Christ in everyone, even in the filthiest person lying in the gutter," she is saying she is aware of a dimension in herself and in others that can't be swept away by the conditions of the moment. She is rooted and knows all of us are rooted in no less than God. She tries to resonate from that level of herself with the same level in others, transcending the pathology and pain of the hour. She can do this because of her personal experience of belonging to that which is eternal. Through years of putting herself into the presence of God, through years of becoming more free as a human being through prayer and spiritual practice, she has learned to serve. Hers is more than psychological coping in a difficult world. It is more than emotional adjustment to the trials and joys of life. She knows that our reality lies in a different, deeper place.

For someone like Mother Teresa, a life of prayerful service is less a life we live than a Life that lives in us. More quickens people like her than a biological will-to-exist or even a psychological will-to-exist-more-happily or an economic will-to-exist-more-successfully. God lives in her. Her service to the world flows from a deeper place than her own solitary action. Those who prayerfully serve may do at least as much or even more than those who work out of their own energy, but paradoxically those who pray and serve do less of the work, for they know that it is God who is the Doer.

God is not a lazy God who created the world and then rested, withdrawing into a distant heaven. God is always with us so that the ground on which we stand, wherever we are, is holy. The radiant light of God's presence is in all things, from the dirt under our feet to the great galaxies flung into infinite space. God is the well of living water, the reservoir of life force just beneath the surface of our lives. That submerged power is like a sunken treasure chest, full of marvels, waiting for us to discover what is there and bring it to the surface. Mostly it lies untouched and neglected, but it is there, filled with love and energy beyond imagining. Being told to serve or being admonished to love doesn't go deeply enough. We learn to love by

103

opening the windows and letting God's life touch the inmost rooms of our souls. When we learn to open ourselves to this Spirit, we find that we serve the world less and less out of our own energy and more and more out of the vast power of God which moves through us to bless and help. God is the Doer. And in that knowledge comes joy.

"We were all created at the same time," says Dame Julian of Norwich, the great fourteenth century English mystic, "and in our creation we were knit and oned to God." When we realize and experience this essential truth, joy takes over from duty.

> For our natural desire is to have God
> and the good desire of God is to have us.
> We can never stop this desire or longing
> until we have our Lover
> in the fullness of joy.[4]

When people know something of this joy, they embrace the whole world. They serve not because they expect anything or are forced to act with dutiful kindness but because that is the essence of their being, like the shining of a star or the blossoming of a tree. Service like this is the spontaneous outflow of divine inner communion.

Dame Julian knew that when we begin to understand our place in God and God's place in all of us, life has a way of coming together. If we hold to the good news of how God and we relate, how we complement each other, how we are vitally one, we will no longer have to force ourselves so much to serve the world. We will need to be admonished less because we are being drawn to God who is so appealing that, for all of the world's garbage, we are moved to seek and serve the Beloved in the world. As God becomes more real to us, loving our neighbors becomes more natural. We no longer think of others as so separate from us; whatever our imperfections and theirs, we are joined by the Life that is in us all. Loving the light that is God, we love it whenever we catch glimpses of it—and yes, in ourselves as well.

Slowly, as we spend time with God, we find that we are moving into a larger picture, passing beyond our own limited perspectives. It comes to us that it is not enough to love just ourselves and those in our immediate circle. We are beginning to see in universals because God is universal. We learn sympathy with the sufferings of others because we are no longer so encased by our own sufferings. We may suffer, but we know that there is more to living than suffering. We want to help others move through the shadows, too, so that all may experience the beauty of God.

There are many ways to move in this direction. Often social liberation must take place before or alongside of personal liberation. Gustavo Gutierrez, an important spokesperson of Latin American liberation theology, says there are three levels of liberation: from oppressive structures of society, from an immobilizing sense of "fate," and from personal sin and guilt.[5] It is not enough to serve individuals out of context; if people are trapped by crushing political and economic conditions, it is imperative to confront and change the principalities and powers that oppress. Still, there are surprises. Personal liberation sometimes has occurred even in the midst of social oppression. Those who are the helpers often find they are also being helped. The poor may have much to teach about life in God being richer than material riches.

Wherever we serve, however God calls each of us, the spiritual life tugs at us to move beyond our impasses. There are social impasses, economic impasses and personal impasses. It is not hard, in a world like this, to become discouraged—to believe there is no way beyond them, no road beyond that which imprisons. These are formidable, tough realities but they don't have the last word. When God is present, old categories are exploded. God is a pulsing heart which can revivify old blood and dead tissue. God is the river of life that spills over dams which no longer serve a useful purpose. God is joy. God breaks out of tombs. Social and personal changes are not easy; sometimes they are painfully hard and involve much suffering. But when we are willing to confess that the power of God is more powerful than we often care to admit and when we give ourselves over to its mystery, divine energy is unshackled and can move stones from our graves.

What is fundamental is whether we really believe in God's power to transform human life. Is our religion mostly entertainment or is it personally and socially powerful? Do we really expect God to work with us or do we assign God the role of "Heavenly Moralizer," the One who lays on rules and regulations but gives no real help that will inspire our efforts from within and bear us up in our struggles?

Our question in this chapter is how service to the world is to be inspired and sustained. If, as I believe is the case, much of our action stems out of what is false in us—heavy layers of envy, compulsion and defensiveness—then it is imperative that we find ways to open up to God's love which lives in the deepest part of ourselves under the layers of the false-self system. On one hand, as Reinhold Niebuhr knew so well, human nature needs constant checks and balances if justice is to be served in even a proximate way. On the other hand, service has to start and end with prayer. Only prayer opens the door to the deepest reservoirs of grace. It is when we are spiritually aware and disciplined that we become open for inner transformation and open to God's work through us for others. Our task is to let loose of our agendas as well as we can (while being honest about what we cling to) and let as much of the love and energy of God the Doer come forth as we can.

The best way to understand this is to experience it. Perhaps you will try the following spiritual exercise—or something like it of your own devising—as a way to open yourself, in the Spirit, to the world. It is a Tibetan Buddhist exercise adapted by Joanna Rogers Macy.

> *Relax. Center on your breathing. . . . Visualize your breath as a stream flowing up through your nose, down through windpipe, lungs. Take it down through your lungs and, picturing an opening in the bottom of your heart, visualize the breath-stream passing through your*

heart and out through that opening to reconnect with the larger web of life around you. Let the breath-stream, as it passes through you, appear as one loop within that vast web, connecting you with it. . . .

Now, open your awareness to the suffering that is present in the world. . . . Let it come as concretely as you can . . . concrete images of your fellow beings in pain and need, in fear and isolation, in prisons, hospitals, tenements, refugee camps. . . . Relax and just let them surface, breathe them in, breathe them through . . . the numberless hardships of our fellow humans and of our animal brothers and sisters. . . . Breathe in that pain like a dark stream, up through your nose, down through your lungs and heart and out again into the world net. . . . Do nothing but let it pass through your heart. . . . Don't hang on to it. . . . Keep breathing. . . . Be sure that stream flows through and out again; don't hang on to the pain. Surrender it for now to the healing resources of life's vast web. . . .

With Shantideva, the Buddhist saint, we can say, "Let all sorrows ripen in me." We help them ripen by passing them through our hearts . . . making good compost out of all that grief. . . .

If you experience an ache in the chest, a pressure within the rib cage, that is all right. The heart that breaks open can contain the whole universe. Your heart is that large. Trust it. Keep breathing. . . .[6]

THE INTERIOR
CASTLE

God is searching for us, pulling us home from our bewilderment. God speaks through many voices to tell us so. God appears in the moon and the stars, in green pastures and by still waters. God comes through the iron rod of Assyria to return his people to justice. God breaks bread with us as Jesus eats and drinks with his friends around a common table. God is the father of the prodigal son, joyfully welcoming us even before we pass through the family gates. God is the Divine Mother, touching us in a phrase of music, a perfect sunset, an empathetic hug from a friend. God finds a thousand ways to tell us we are sought after.

Just as God searches for us, we search for God. Our souls are designed for the infinite. We may try to settle for less but we never quite pull it off. Even in the midst of our jobs it is never enough for us to labor without purpose; we want to be renewed by and serve through our work as well as make a living at it, and if that doesn't happen, our souls tug at us. When we play they tug, too, pulling us into the goodness of each moment as we enjoy our families or as we take in what rises before us when a mountain comes up over the horizon while we drive. Each person's soul demands satisfaction. The search pattern within us casts about, looking for no less than our divine connection. When we try to ignore that or stamp it out, we are restless and bent out of shape.

Much of the time our search for God occurs as formless groping. It takes many shapes but, however disguised, it occurs constantly. People on drugs may be trying to shut out pain, but they are also searching for meaning, however distorted. People who attend concerts are usually searching for something just behind the music—an encounter with the divine core of life, a kind of lower-case mystical experience.

What I have tried to point to in this book is the serious (though often joyful) nature of this search when it moves from groping to intention. We find that the spiritual journey is no quick-fix. Sister Moriah, a nun in the Episcopal Order of Saint Anne, tells about having gone from the tepid Protestantism of her girlhood to atheism to fundamentalism. And then she made a discovery. She thought she had arrived when she moved into the "extroverted spirituality of fundamentalism," only to see that her journey had just begun.

> The reborn thing seems to stop. You're reborn, you're saved . . . and you don't need to deepen anything. In fundamentalist circles, there isn't much of an emphasis on a personal search, a personal journey, on going ever deeper into yourself and the mystery of God. And I'm not sure anyone can be satisfied with that for very long.[1]

Sister Moriah discovered what many people on the spiritual journey find. Not only is the journey no quick-fix but it is intended to take us into far greater and far richer places than we might have believed. It is the witness of the saints that this journey is concerned with nothing less than a movement into ever higher levels of reality until there is an at-one-ment with the God of love who wishes to share divine life with us. This is far different than the popular images of the human journey which tell us that we exist to become beautiful people, or nicer people, or that we are here on earth to acquire a station wagon and a sports car in every garage (or whatever the current fad may be).

While each person's journey is unique, there are constant themes that reoccur in the lives of the spiritual giants:

> The journey of the spirit is like coming home. It is a return to normalcy, so that when such normalcy is experienced, everything less than being lived in God seems subnormal by comparison.

It involves purification, a cleaning out of that which is less than God. All secondary desires are redirected.

The journey is a journey into divine love. During this journey, God becomes experienced and not just explored as an object of intellectual inquiry.

This journey is what human existence is all about. It's why we're alive. As we travel through it, we come home not only to God but to ourselves.

When God's radiant love is given room to expand our souls and minds, we don't have to be told about this journey; we know. I resonate to the haiku of a friend, Jim Grob, because Jim has experienced God's presence and purpose for himself and puts the journey into the language of the heart:

God fires the oven
I—dough, bake, rise and brown
My me becomes He

St. Teresa of Avila is being rediscovered in our time because she personally experienced this journey and is able to give us a powerful feel for it. In her celebrated *The Interior Castle*, she speaks with great passion and practicality about the way to God. Using glorious metaphors and drawing on her own hard-won experience, she says that this journey is like moving more and more deeply into the interior of an extremely beautiful crystal castle which is filled with many rooms through which we must pass before reaching the innermost chamber, the place of full communion with God.

Teresa says that the journey starts when we begin to find that life isn't as great outside the castle as we had thought. There, at the outside, are crawling, dark things, symbols of what life is like when we are alienated from ourselves and the castle's King. Tired finally of being so absorbed with everything but the One who waits for us, we enter the castle to find it consists of many rooms arranged around the center where

God's light is all in all. Once we enter we find we also come home.

> Well, getting back to our beautiful and delightful castle we must see how we can enter it. It seems I'm saying something foolish. For if this castle is the soul, clearly one doesn't have to enter it since it is within oneself. How foolish it would seem were we to tell someone to enter a room he is already in.[2]

In the first rooms dwell those who are starting to hear God's voice among the many distractions of life. The heat and light from the center of the castle are as present here as at the center, but the soul is still so disoriented and fractured that it continues to be drawn in countless directions. Still, she prays and takes stock of herself occasionally and is beginning to sense that she has been occupied with everything but her interior life.

> It's as if a person were to enter a place where the sun is shining but be hardly able to open his eyes because of the mud in them. The room is bright but he doesn't enjoy it because of the impediment of things like these wild animals or beasts that make him close his eyes to everything but them.[3]

In the second mansions or rooms, God's voice is clearer. The soul is more aware of being challenged to reorient her life around a truer center. She is beginning to hear the King more frequently through inspiring books, sermons, the company of good people, illnesses and trials. But she is still very resistant and allows herself to be pulled from one distraction to another.

In the third mansions, the soul moves into an intentional spiritual place. Life begins to become ordered around a divine core and there is energy for serious prayer and charity. Teresa says that many "mature Christians" live here and many think that this is where the spiritual life is supposed to conclude.

Because of her own experience, she disagrees totally. Teresa insists that the spiritual life has just been launched, that the best things are ahead, and those at this level must move on. In my own experience, it is precisely at this third level that the contemporary church loses its way. We teach people that the spiritual life is the same as dedicated service to the world and the church—and certainly these matter—but we seldom tell them there is so much more to be uncovered. Perhaps it is because so few of our clergy have themselves been awakened or led into deeper spiritual places. The truth is, in the third rooms the journey has just begun!

> To overstay in the third dwelling place may lead to danger-ous and difficult times. An anxiety may creep into these model lives. Prayer loses its vitality; a dryness sets in. . . . These people try to do more of what they had been doing, in the belief that what has worked in the past will work now. . . . Teresa's diagnosis is that these apparently model Christians have not really abandoned themselves. . . . The signs indicate that they are being asked to let go of this stability, to move out of the third dwelling place and allow the King at the center to draw them ever deeper into the castle.[4]

It is in the fourth, fifth and sixth mansions that the connection with God becomes more solid and firmed up. In the fourth mansion, the Spirit assumes a more visible role by drawing the soul to a quieter, more receptive place, sometimes taking it into moments when it is powerfully conscious of God's self-communication to it as a beloved friend. In the peace of God's presence, a deep happiness sets in—even when life is hard.

This fourth stage is a turning point. Until now, although the grace of God has been fully at work, the spotlight has been on us and our responsibility for getting on with the journey, as though God has been waiting to see how serious we are. Now, God's role is more visible.

Let's consider, for a better understanding, that we see two founts with two water troughs. . . . These two troughs are filled with water in different ways; with one the water comes from far away through many aqueducts and the use of much ingenuity; with the other the source of water is right there, and the trough fills without any noise. . . . There is no need of any skill, nor does the building of aqueducts have to continue; but water is always flowing from the spring. . . . With this . . . fount, the water comes from its own source, which is God. . . . He produces this delight with the greatest peace and quiet and sweetness in the very interior part of ourselves.[5]

In the fifth mansion, God increasingly unites a person with himself so powerfully and deeply that for a brief period of time she may be aware of little else. Because the experience of God is so good, it leads to a stronger and stronger desire to live for God alone and to enjoy and serve the Gracious One.

By the sixth stage union is prolonged. It is also a time of further cleansing. God is at work enlarging the soul. There may be many trials both exterior and interior. It takes great courage to proceed. Sometimes God seems to have disappeared and the soul feels as if she is in a desert. At other times, just one word from the King and she is flooded with waters which quench every thirst. There is increasing clarity, light and joy, but if the soul stays properly attuned, whatever the phenomena she may or may not experience, she is clear that she wants to live for God who is good beyond all she could imagine.

The seventh stage is a wonderful homecoming. The soul is one with God. Deep interior peace is a constant state. The divine indwelling promised in John 14:23 in which Christ says "My Father and I will come to him and live with him" is continually experienced.

And the union is also different because, even though it is the joining of two things into one, in the end the two can be separated and each remains by itself. . . . Let us say that the union is like the joining of two wax candles to such an extent that the flame coming from them is but one, or that the wick, the flame, and the wax are all one. But afterward one candle can be easily separated from the other and there are two candles; the same holds for the wick. . . . Or it is like what we have when a little stream enters the sea, and there is no means of separating the two. Or, like the bright light entering a room through two different windows; although the streams of light are separate when entering the room, they become one. Perhaps this is what Saint Paul means in saying *He that is joined or united to the Lord becomes one spirit with him. . . .*[6]

In this place of union, this homecoming, the soul is so firmly anchored that no matter the circumstance, nothing can disturb her joy. She has let go of her compulsions and illusions. Her desire is simple and single—to live in the presence of God and to serve God wherever she lives. Her life is Christ, and as with Christ, the purpose of this splendid journey to the interior is to move back to the exterior so that nothing less than God's love can be known within and offered to all. The fruit of spiritual marriage is good works.

How compelling it is to journey with Teresa into the interior of the castle! Hers is personal testimony; she speaks from experience and her words ring with authenticity. How we want to join her in this journey—and how we pause at the gates! Our fears surface. "We'll lose control," we warn ourselves.

It is true that another Life takes "control" as we move to the interior of the castle, but it doesn't do away with us; it fulfills us. Teresa's castle is an image of wholeness; it is a metaphor of the fullness of life that can be found when people travel inward to the Self. It is a journey of transformations. As Carl Jung knew, in the first stages of life the Spirit is shaping us in the direction of gaining identity and discovering our roles and abilities. In the later stages of life, as we enter mid-life and beyond, we seem to be designed to let go and open up to richer realities within. In both stages we are meant to become more individuated which means at the same time drawn to that center within where the Spirit of God and the soul of man touch, and drawn to be more human.

This is a journey of convergence where being fully human and being God's person comes together. As God is more fully expressed through us, the more our personalities expand toward their potential. The more we expand our potential, the more the Divine Life is radiating outward to achieve its purposes.

Dare we take this journey? As far as I can tell from my own experience and from that of many others, there comes a time when we find we can't put it off any longer. That which is healthy in us insists on its own way. We know that such a journey is the only path left if we are to mature.

And so we take the hand of God.

When we face our ambiguities about really going for the spiritual life, one's own experiences carry a lot more freight than philosophical argument. The early Christians could face Roman persecution, not because they were admonished to be spiritual, but because they had met Christ face to face. This happens to us all. Sometimes it is a quiet thing. Sometimes it is more riveting. Such moments stay with us and carry us forward.

A few years ago, on Holy Saturday—the day between Good Friday and Easter—I was on a day-long retreat with thirty other people. I had no other responsibility than to be as open to God as I could.

God was there—abundantly! The day was filled with holy Presence.

In that holy and loving Presence, things became very clear and very simple. God is. God is closer than our living and breathing. We swim in an ocean of spirit every moment; it's just that mostly we grope around at the bottom of the ocean instead of at the surface where sunlight meets wave. That day I was open and conscious enough to know that I, and all that is, was bathed by the light. It is always there but for some gracious reason on that occasion I was able to experience it more than usual. Besides the Presence, I was also particularly aware of the garbage I carry around in me. Though that garbage was even more painfully apparent than usual, against the light it had no more reality than a bank of clouds. It was the "sun" that ultimately mattered and which gave off love, warmth and encouragement beyond saying. And yet that experience of God was as ordinary as could be—the most normal thing in the universe.

I still carry that experience with me. In that holy Presence I was open and wanted to open up more, and it reminds me how good it is to open when I don't. I saw reality more clearly, and when I don't see it so well, I remember what it is like.

God's goodness is right here. Somehow we have gotten it in our heads that there isn't enough of that goodness to go around and that we have to hoard what we have. We believe we have to guard ourselves, keep control, fence things off. Of course we have to be sensible and responsible. We have mouths to feed and things to accomplish. But the spiritual life is all about moving into the Presence with the consciousness of generosity rather than fearful anxiety. As that rises in us, we learn that we don't have to close down to be safe. We begin to sense God's hand at work, guiding us. Sometimes, we discover, God opens up fuller perspectives to us, as was the case for me on that retreat. Sometimes God helps us discover what lessons we need to learn as we take our next steps. Sometimes God gives us very down-to-earth blessings as doors are opened to whatever is right for us at this stage of the journey. Sometimes we are in the desert but find that God is there, too, wanting to help us grow.

Probably the most important thing about which to remind ourselves as we move into the castle is that for those who report from its center, the anxiety about whether the trip is worth it is much less apparent than the anxiety of the rest of us! When someone like Teresa reports back, it is clear that she has learned to trust the process! Besides, anyone who knows her story knows how vital, alive and engaging a human being she was—the more so the more she lived in God. She wrote

The Interior Castle to inspire the rest of us to participate in the search for spiritual reality because she knew it was not only the source of her own profound joy but it is the full life that a gracious God intends for all of his children.

Somewhere in her writings, Evelyn Underhill says that for the most part and for most people, the presence of the spiritual universe surrounding us is no more noticed than the pressure of air on our bodies. Our spiritual senses aren't sufficiently alert. We work hard at developing our relationship to the visible world, but our relationship to the spiritual is rudimentary by comparison. The most momentous step forward we humans can make is the step that takes us into an intentional spiritual life. For all the talk in our world about human destiny and progress, this step gets talked about very little. And yet the way of evolution is the way into the interior castle.

The most challenging and important task we humans have is our spiritual development. We avoid it because it threatens us to shift the center of our consciousness to that which lies within from that which is without. Yet history bears witness that God's children have tried everything under the sun and moon to satisfy the hunger that only God himself can fill. In all the universe, there is only one way to gratify this hunger, and that is through the integration of our surface lives with the Divine Self which lives in our depths and to which we are joined.

It boils down to trust.

We need to trust our deepest instincts for the Divine. We need to trust that the same divine pattern that makes up the physical universe is also true of us. Within the pattern of our beings is the image of the living Christ, waiting to come forth. We need to believe it is our destiny to be set free, to follow the elemental nature of life which is to increase and to seek fuller and fuller expression. We need to welcome the truth we are here to express in fullness what we already are potentially. We need to trust our destiny rather than fight it, allowing the Light to come forward and increase. We need to trust our

120

deepest wisdom and the deepest wisdom of the human community which knows we are most complete when the Spirit is consented to.

What is the cosmic drama that is being played out? Jesus says it is like a mustard seed. A mustard seed is far more than a collection of molecules clinging together—an insignificant bit of matter soon to fall into decay. Jesus talked about mustard seeds because he and his listeners knew how tiny those seeds are. To anyone who doesn't know better, it is absurd to imagine that a seed is a divine pattern held in waiting, eager to come forth as a leafy plant which will be high as a tree and large enough to shelter birds in its foliage.

We are human mustard seeds. It is no more obvious to our surface minds what we are than the pattern in a mustard seed is obvious to our naked eye. Yet, as the pattern in the mustard seed is locked within its life force, awaiting proper conditions for release, the Christ pattern is locked within us, awaiting our willingness to let God plant, water and nourish that which God eagerly calls us to become.

That which is deeply wise in us knows the truth. We are here to be in a permanent and abiding communion with the One who calls to us from the center of our souls.

No other journey we take and no other business we pursue holds a candle to the journey into the interior castle.

NOTES

Preface

1. Tilden Edwards, *Living Simply Through the Day* (New York: Paulist Press, 1977), p. 7.
2. Joseph Campbell, *The Power of the Myth* (New York: Doubleday, 1988), p. 15.

Moving Out

1. Gerald G. May, *Will and Spirit* (San Francisco: Harper and Row, 1982), p. 89.
2. C.S. Lewis, *The Great Divorce* (New York: Macmillan Co., 1946), pp. 69–70.
3. John Westerhoff III and John D. Eusden, *The Spiritual Life, Learning East and West* (New York: Seabury Press, 1982), p. 58.

What Draws Us to God?/What Holds Us Back?

1. Thomas R. Kelly, *A Testament of Devotion* (San Francisco: Harper and Row, 1941), pp. 114–115.
2. Peter S. Beagle, *The Last Unicorn* (New York: Ballantine Books, 1968), pp. 8–9.
3. From the jacket cover of Marjorie Holmes' book, *How Can I Find You, God?* (New York: Guideposts, 1975).
4. Elizabeth O'Connor, *Search for Silence* (Waco, Texas: Word Books, 1972), pp. 114–115.
5. Frederick Buechner, "Summons to Pilgrimage," quoted by Elizabeth O'Connor in *Search for Silence*, p. 178.

Coming to God As We Are

1. John Powell, *He Touched Me* (Allen, Texas: Argus Communications, 1974), pp. 63–66.
2. Anthony Bloom, *Beginning To Pray* (New York: Paulist Press, 1970), p. 49.
3. *Ibid.*, pp. 49–50.

Listening

1. Katherine Dyckman and Patrick Carroll, *Inviting the Mystic, Supporting the Prophet* (New York: Paulist Press, 1981), pp. 34–35.
2. Powell, *He Touched Me*, pp. 74–75.

Growth

1. American Psychoanalytic Association, "About Psychoanalysis" (a pamphlet published in 1985), p. 1.

Attunement

1. Swami Kriyananda, "A New Dispensation" (a pamphlet published by Ananda Press, Nevada City), pp. 4–5.
2. Brother Lawrence, *The Practice of the Presence of God* (Cincinnati: Forward Movement Press, 1981), pp. 29–30.
3. R.M. French, trans., *The Way of a Pilgrim* (New York: Seabury Press, 1965), p. v.
4. Sri Daya Mata, *Self-Realization Magazine* (Winter Issue, 1983), p. 50.

Meditation, the Way of Inner Communion

1. Bloom, *Beginning To Pray*, pp. 93–94.
2. Thomas Keating, "Contemplative Prayer in Christian Tradition," in *Finding Grace at the Center* (Petersham: St. Bede Press, 1978), p. 45.
3. *Ibid.*, p. 36.

4. Henry Suso quoted in *Mysticism* by Evelyn Underhill (London: Methuen Press, 1955), p. 187.
5. From Pascal's Memorial as quoted by Ernest Mortimer in *Blaise Pascal* (Darby, Pa: Folcroft Library Services, 1979), p. 123.
6. Fritjof Capra, *The Tao of Physics* (New York: Bantam, 1984), p. 11.
7. Thomas Keating, *Open Mind, Open Heart* (Warwick: Amity House, 1986), pp. 136–137.

Service

1. Tilden Edwards, ed., *Living with Apocalypse, Spiritual Resources for Social Compassion* (San Francisco: Harper and Row, 1984), p. 16.
2. *Ibid.*, p. 17.
3. Taylor Branch, *Parting the Waters: America in the King Years 1954–63* (New York: Simon and Schuster, 1988), p. 162.
4. Brendan Doyle, *Meditations with Julian of Norwich* (Santa Fe: Bear and Company, 1983), p. 31.
5. Letty M. Russell, "Issues in Liberation Theology," *Yale Divinity School Reflections* (Winter 1986), p. 13.
6. Edwards, *Living with Apocalypse*, pp. 126–127.

The Interior Castle

1. Norman Boucher, "Spiritual Hunger in America," *New Age Journal* (April 1986), p. 75.
2. Kieran Kavanaugh and Otilio Rodriguez, trans., *Teresa of Avila, The Interior Castle* (New York: Paulist Press, 1979), p. 37.
3. *Ibid.*, p. 45.
4. John Welch, *Spiritual Pilgrims, Carl Jung and Teresa of Avila* (New York: Paulist Press, 1982), p. 18.
5. Kavanaugh and Rodriguez, *Teresa of Avila*, p. 74.
6. *Ibid.*, p. 179.

BIBLIOGRAPHY

Abishiktananda (Fr. Henri Le Saux, OSB). *Prayer*. Philadelphia: Westminster Press, 1973.

A Monk of the Eastern Church. *Orthodox Spirituality: An Outline of the Orthodox Ascetical and Mystical Tradition*. Crestwood, N.Y.: St. Vladimir's Seminary Press, 1978.

Barry, William A. and William J. Connolly. *The Practice of Spiritual Direction*. New York: Seabury, 1982.

Bloom, Anthony. *Beginning To Pray*. New York: Paulist Press, 1970.

DelBene, Ron. *The Breath of Life, A Simple Way To Pray*. Minneapolis, Winston Press, 1981.

de Mello, Anthony. *Wellsprings*. Garden City: Doubleday, 1985.

Carroll, Patrick and Catherine Dyckman. *Inviting the Mystic, Supporting the Prophet, An Introduction to Spiritual Direction*. New York: Paulist Press, 1981.

————. *Chaos or Creation, Spirituality in Mid-Life*. New York: Paulist Press, 1986.

Dorr, Donald. *Spirituality and Justice*. New York: Orbis, 1984.

Edwards, Tilden. *Living Simply Through the Day*. New York: Paulist Press, 1977.

————, ed. *Living with Apocalypse*. San Francisco: Harper and Row, 1984.

————. *Spiritual Friend. Reclaiming the Gift of Spiritual Direction*. New York: Paulist Press, 1980.

Egan, Harvey. *Christian Mysticism: The Future of a Tradition*. New York: Pueblo Publishing, 1984.

Fischer, Kathleen. *Women at the Well: Feminist Perspectives on Spiritual Direction.* New York: Paulist Press, 1988.

Foster, Richard. *Celebration of Discipline: Paths to Spiritual Growth.* San Francisco: Harper and Row, 1978.

Fowler, James. *Stages of Faith.* New York: Harper and Row, 1981.

Fox, Matthew. *Original Blessing.* Santa Fe: Bear and Company, 1983.

French, R.M., trans. *The Way of a Pilgrim and The Pilgrim Continues His Way.* Minneapolis: Seabury, 1952.

Gyanamata, Sri. *God Alone.* Los Angeles: Self Realization Fellowship, 1984.

Helleberg, Marilyn. *Beyond TM: A Practical Guide to the Lost Traditions of Christian Meditation.* New York: Paulist Press, 1980.

Herbert, George. *The Poems of George Herbert.* New York: AMS Press, reprint of 1907 edition.

Holmes, Urban. *A History of Christian Spirituality.* New York: Seabury, 1981.

John of the Cross, Saint. *The Collected Works of St. John of the Cross.* Trans. Kieran Kavanaugh and Otto Rodriguez. Washington: Institute of Carmelite Studies, 1964.

Johnston, William, ed. *The Cloud of the Unknowing and The Book of Privy Counseling.* Garden City: Doubleday and Co., Image Books, 1973.

Jones, Alan. *Soul Making: The Desert Way of Spirituality.* San Francisco: Harper and Row, 1985.

Keating, Thomas. *Open Mind, Open Heart.* New York: Amity House, 1986.

Kelly, Thomas. *A Testament of Devotion.* San Francisco: Harper and Row, 1941.

Kelsey, Morton. *The Other Side of Silence.* New York: Paulist Press, 1976.

Kriyananda, Swami. *The Path.* Nevada City: Ananda Press, 1979.

Lawrence of the Resurrection, Brother. *The Practice of the Presence of God.* New York: Paulist Press, 1978.

Laubach, Frank. *Letters by a Modern Mystic*. Syracuse: New Reader's Press, 1979.

Leckey, Delores. *The Ordinary Way: A Family Spirituality*. New York: Crossroad, 1982.

Leech, Kenneth. *Soul Friend: The Practice of Christian Spirituality*. San Francisco: Harper and Row, 1982.

Macy, Joanna Rogers. *Despair and Personal Power in the Nuclear Age*. Philadelphia: New Society, 1983.

Main, John. *In the Stillness Dancing*. New York: Crossroad, 1986.

May, Gerald. *Addiction and Grace*. San Francisco: Harper and Row, 1988.

————. *Will and Spirit: Toward a Contemplative Psychology*. San Francisco: Harper and Row, 1982.

McNamara, William. *Christian Mysticism: A Psychotheology*. Chicago: Franciscan Herald Press, 1981.

Merton, Thomas. *New Seeds of Contemplation*. New York: New Directions, 1972.

Mott, Michael. *The Seven Mountains of Thomas Merton*. Boston: Houghton Mifflin, 1984.

Nemeck, Francis and Marie Theresa Coombs. *Contemplation*. Wilmington: Michael Glazier, Inc., 1980.

Nouwen, Henry. *The Way of the Heart*. New York: Crossroad, 1981.

O'Connor, Elizabeth. *Search for Silence*. Waco: Word Books, 1972.

Peck, M. Scott. *The Road Less Traveled*. New York: Simon and Schuster, 1978.

Pennington, M. Basil. *Centered Living: The Way of Centering Prayer*. Garden City: Doubleday, 1986.

Powell, John. *He Touched Me*. Allen, Texas: Argus, 1974.

Rogers, Barbara. *In the Center, The Story of a Retreat*. Notre Dame: Ave Maria Press, 1983.

Sanford, John. *The Kingdom Within: The Inner Meaning of Jesus' Sayings*, Videocassette. New York: Paulist Press, 1983.

Senn, Frank, ed. *Protestant Spiritual Traditions*. New York: Paulist Press, 1986.

Steere, Douglas. *Together in Solitude*. San Francisco: Harper and Row, 1985.

Teresa of Avila. *The Interior Castle* (trans. Kieran Kavanaugh and Otilio Rodriguez). New York: Paulist Press, 1979.

Trungpa, Chogyam. *Cutting Through Spiritual Materialism*. Boston: Shambhala Publications, 1973.

Tulka, Tarthang. *Gesture of Balance: A Guide to Awareness, Self-Healing and Meditation*. California: Dharma Publications, 1976.

Underhill, Evelyn. *Mysticism*. New York: E.P. Dutton, 1961.

Wakefield, Gordon, ed. *The Westminster Dictionary of Christian Spirituality*. Philadelphia: Westminster Press, 1983.

Walker, Alice. *The Color Purple*. New York: Harcourt, Brace, Jovanovich, 1982.

Ward, Benedicta, trans. *The Sayings of the Desert Fathers: The Alphabetical Collection*. Kalamazoo, Mich.: Cistercian Publications, 1975.

Walker, Susan, ed. *Speaking of Silence, Christians and Buddhists on the Contemplative Way*. New York: Paulist Press, 1987.

Welch, John. *Spiritual Pilgrims, Carl Jung and Teresa of Avila*. New York: Paulist Press, 1982.

Yogananda, Paramahansa. *Autobiography of a Yogi*. Los Angeles: Self-Realization Fellowship, 1946.